ENTRAPMENT IN BLOOD

Rodriguez Bros.

vs.

United States of America

-

JOSEPH RODRIGUEZ

JourStarr Quality Publications LLC

Copyright © 2017 Joseph Rodriguez

Published by
'JourStarr Quality Publications
P.O. Box 6233
Wheeling WV, 26003

ISBN-10: 0-9971524-5-1
ISBN-13: 978-0-9971524-5-6

Library of Congress Control Number:
2017955892

Letter To My Readers:

Dear Reader, This book asks, "Where is Justice?" Was justice done in this case? Was the government's evidence strong enough for a life sentence? It gives you a chance to put yourself in the jury's seat. Would you have believed Mr. Flores, the government's key witness? Did the FBI go too far with the Rest Stop set up? A lot of things are not right with this case. Why care? Next time it may be you or someone you care about that encounters this kind of injustice.

I hope you enjoy this book. It was a very difficult task for me to document my entire case. I experienced a lot of pain, as past emotions were relived to pull all the facts together for you. Hopefully, in some way it will upset you also. To the point that you will want to bring the truth to light. (Not my story, the truth, good or bad.)

No matter how you feel after reading this book, if you would like to see any of the statements or reports or anything dealing with this case, please write me at the address listed below.

Thank you for your time.

Sincerely,
Joseph Rodriguez

P.S. Please feel free to share this book with anyone that may be able to help. "The Truth is Out There"

SEND TO:
Joseph Rodriguez/ USP 20260-050
P.O. Box 300
WAYMART, PA 18472

Prologue:

This book is about a failed assassination attempt by the F.B.I., to murder three men. On September 1, 1998 the F.B.I, set up the Rodriguez brothers (Charles and Joe) along with their friend Jose Soto with an armor truck robbery worth one million dollars in cash.

This case has been aired on a F.B.I, crime show more than twenty times. An American crime show aired Charles story three times. Many TV news and newspapers have featured this case.

It's been over ten years and the truth has not come to light. If you want to read about a real injustice and how far the F.B.I, went to set them up. Then read this book and your eyes will open.

The Rodriguez brothers are ready to share any statements, lab reports and trial transcripts. They want you to put yourself in the juror's seat. Would you have believed the government's key witness Fernando Flores, enough to sentence the Rodriguez brothers and Soto to life in prison?

Acknowledgements

I would like to give thanks to all the guys in the library that helped me when I needed it; too many to mention. Some helped me in little ways and others guided me along the way.

Special thanks to our family, such as our big sister Marissa, Carmen, and our nephews. Also thanks to all the families for the support and financial contributions to this book. To our little sister Carmen, you have been our secretary, mailman, and banker; go to person and our 411 on everything we asked for.

You have made this hard time in this crazy place a little bit easier. For that we will always be thankful to you. Thanks sis for everything.

We Love You All Mucho, Mucho.

Charles/Joe This book is dedicated to our mother Edith, who passed away July 12, 2010. You will be missed deeply. We love you so much. God Bless You, Mom

Chapter 1

It was a crisp fall day. The sky was blue and the sun spread its warm rays to dull the brisk September air. For the general public, life this day was as any other day. As people made their way north and southbound along the New Jersey Turnpike in effort to arrive to work on time, the hustle and bustle of everyday commutes flowed fluidly. Right near Exit Four on the turnpike, the Walt Whitman Service Plaza stood. We approached the plaza from the north end of the service road. There were no toll booths on that side of the freeway, so it made things easier for us to unnoticeably access the rear entrance of the service plaza.

Creeping up the service road was my cousin, Fernando Flores. As his baseball cap covered his big head, there he was in the driver's seat of a Buick, which had been stolen from Philadelphia. My brother, Charles Rodriguez, sat in the back seat directly behind Fernando. I sat in the front on the passenger's side, right across from Fernando, and my friend of many years, Jose Soto, was in the back seat, positioned directly behind me.

For us, the day was totally out of the ordinary. Of course, I was nervous. We all were. It was go time, and while driving up the long windy road of the rear service entrance, our pulses sped up and our heart beats increased out of anticipation. My body temperature was rising. The red windbreaker I was wearing covered the heavy gear I had strapped to my body. I felt the heat under my collar, as perspiration condensed under my armpits.

Jose and Charlie had on their black military style apparel. Actually, we all wore the same bothersome gear, and underneath their threads, I would safely bet that they felt the same as I did. If that wasn't the case, I at least hoped Fernando was hot under his collar. I mean it was his brilliant idea to wear all that gear in the first place. Therefore, he deserved to suffer for that crazy suggestion.

We neared a dirt road that broke off towards the side, which led us into a lot of greenery. The side road diverted down to a lone house, which was hidden in some trees. As we passed the small road, there was a midsized tow truck parked in front of the solemn house. Charlie noticed it first, because it sat facing us.

"That's funny", Charlie said. "Looks like somebody's sitting in the front seat of that truck."

The atmosphere was already uncomfortable, but the presence of the truck instigated a feeling of foreboding that suddenly felt heavy upon our shoulders. Looking back at it now, there's no question that the vehicle was the first sign of the trouble events to come. Still, as stubborn as we were, we continued with our plan.

Once we reached the top of the service road, we entered the rear parking lot of the rest stop. Strangely enough, it was odd that a service plaza was located alongside a freeway, but the parking lot was barren, almost as if we'd driven ourselves into a ghost town. Only a lone pickup truck could be seen. As we entered the lot, the truck was positioned immediately to our right. Fernando decided to back into the parking space directly next to the truck and park.

Surveying the area, we could see the main building of the service plaza. It was positioned directly across from our position, standing at a right angle. As we entered the area, a grassy patch stretched from the main building to the left, disappearing into the trees that had accompanied us up the service road. On the other side of the patch was the front parking lot. Of course, we couldn't see the front parking area, our view was obscured by the few scattered trees and the rear of the smaller structure constructed next to the main building.

The building itself was positioned at an angle and from our position in the parking lot; the trees covered most of the building from our view. Several of the windows were in sight. One of the windows portrayed a silhouetted image of a person watching us.

The second warning is the guy in the window. We noticed that the same tow truck was somehow a little closer to the parking lot entrance. Originally, the plan was for Fernando to get out of the car and walk across the lot. He was supposed to cross over the grass and walk to some pay phones next to the smaller building. Fernando quietly reached for the door handle to get out of the car, but my brother Charlie interrupted him.

"Hold up. Stay in the car. This don't look good. Let's drive around to the front of the building."

In all actuality, Charlie wanted to leave the parking lot area all together. Yet, unfortunately, the tow truck made its way up the road far enough to block the lots rear entrance. Driving to the front of the parking lot was our only option, so we pulled the car away from the space we were occupying and continued driving farther into the lot. I felt like I was like looking down a long football field, only there was no football game taking place, and the field was covered with blacktop. I looked back and I could see that the tow truck had halted its advancement, and was now completely blocking the parking entrance. I told myself, something was definitely wrong.

We slowly eased southbound towards the end of the main building. In the open space ahead of us, we could see how far the rest stop parking lot stretched to the south east. At the corner of the building, we followed the black top, as it softly curved to the left. We followed the driveway around the building to the east end lot, which was towards the front. When we cleared the bend, two white vans faced us. They were parked as if they were about to execute an ambush. A lump of fear consumed my throat, but the closer we got, the more the vans seemed vacant.

The nervous energy among all of us in the car grew thick. The alarm bells screamed frantically within my head. Still, we weren't a hundred percent sure if we had driven ourselves into a trap, or if we were just being extremely paranoid. There were many telltale signs that set the scene around us, making us very wary of our situation, yet we were not able to confirm exactly what was about to take place.

"I don't like this," Charlie simply said.

When we passed the two vans, nothing happened. Feeling a little more comfortable, we followed the path that led along the top end of the main building. The trail was right next to where the front parking lot opened completely up to reveal the other side of the freeway. It was diagonally to our right. Sadly, we could see a lonely island of gas pumps that awaited customers who would surely not arrive that day. Finally, we rounded the bend of the side walk, slowly passing the gas pumps...

Chapter 2

This is a story about two brothers; my brother, Charlie Rodriguez and me, Joseph Rodriguez. We were both born and raised in South Camden, New Jersey. Through the years, we definitely experienced our share of drama. Like any kid raised in a rough neighborhood, we learned to survive on the streets. Charlie, who was older than me by one year, was constantly in and out of trouble with the law. Charlie had a budding reputation in our area. I, on the other hand, was a little more discreet. Unfortunately, in the late 80's through the early 90's, I had been placed in my brother's shadow and was suspected of participating in a string of armed home invasions throughout the Camden area. The targeted hits were drug dealers.

Evidence was never sufficient enough to link me or Charlie to any of the home invasions. Although charges were never filed, and a conviction was never secured from the police investigation, Charlie remained a must grab on the authorities' radar. The streets of Camden are a haven for the various types of underworld ventures. It's a breeding ground for addiction and violence; not to mention that sex and drugs are a main source of income for many of the residents.

In November of 1989, the police indulged in their vendetta against Charlie. Edward Lopez, a thirty-two year old man from North Camden, was gunned down during a drive-by shooting in his own area. The shooting was believed to be part of a war between rival drug gangs from North and East Camden. The "rival drug gang" theory was concocted by local media. As far as I know, the real reason for the shooting was never publically revealed.

Authorities used the shooting as an opportunity to arrest my brother. On November 14, 1989, Charlie was officially charged for the murder of Eduardo Lopez. Two additional charges of aggravated assault were also lodged against Charlie, because bystanders were injured during the shooting.

Fortunately, Charlie pled not guilty to all counts; and in May of 1992, three years after the shooting of Lopez, my brother was found not guilty on all charges.

The Camden County Police were irate about the verdict. However, after the acquittal, Charlie's name stayed out of the papers for a good while, and he didn't experience any run-ins with the law. Still, the police made it a point to continually surveillance him. As far as they were concerned, Charlie had eluded them twice. Once with the home invasion investigation, and then again with the Lopez murder trial. They wanted Charlie to be guilty of all those acts, yet the evidence always proved otherwise. Therefore, that didn't sit well with the authorities. When Charlie finally came in contact with the police again, the circumstances weren't quite what they'd hoped for. Turns out that Charlie was the victim, but the police weren't really on his side.

In the fall of 1996, on November 4, Charlie was shot in the face by an unknown assailant as he stood on the corner of Beckett and White Streets. The bullet entered through Charlie's right temple from a gunman who fired from only a few feet away. Miraculously, it deflected downward at an angle. The bullet passed through the inside of his mouth and exited out through the back of his left jaw, shattering it completely. My brother suffered through reconstructive surgery, and his jaw had to be wired together. He was miserable for months afterwards, but he survived.

Charlie's run-ins with the law were usually typical like with most street thugs. Authorities found him in possession of a firearm, discovered that he threatened a witness once, and knew that he loved to smoke weed, so he had to face some drug paraphernalia charges. To some people, those things might seem serious, but in our neighborhood, it was just part of our day-to-day routine. It could never be said, or proven that Charlie had ever been involved in any dramatic life altering situations, excluding him being shot. However, there were those who wished to prove otherwise.

As for me, I was less prevalent in the news papers. I always held a steady job, so my experiences with the law were less extensive than that of my brother. I was also suspected, alongside of Charlie, during the late 80's, early 90's of being involved with those home invasions. As I said before, nothing had ever come of that investigation. Nothing that is, until the year of 1991. In May of 1991, I was arrested for murder, felony murder, burglary, assault, etc. A man named Luis Rivera was killed during one such home invasion. I can tell you now that I never physically shot anyone, but I can be man enough to take responsibility for my part in the robbery.

It turned out to be a very messy case. My brother had never been charged with that particular home invasion, but I was. I was drug through very complicated and highly frustrating court proceedings. Initially, I pled not guilty and took the case to trial. After an exhausting trial that ended with a hung jury, I was worn out. My co-defendants in that case had already pled guilty to the crime. When I took the case to trial, my co-defendants testified that I had nothing to do with the situation. Ultimately, their testimony pushed the jury to be undecided. The prosecution was furious and relentlessly pushed for a retrial, as should be done in such case. The authorities turned up the heat on me by threatening to take the plea agreements from my co-defendants and giving them a full thirty year sentence. I didn't want my friends to do all that time because of me. A man was killed that night, and that will forever be my greatest regret

So, in 1995, after four years of exhausting court battles, I finally pled guilty to a lesser charge of manslaughter, "The plea held five to fifteen years." I wasn't proud of my decision, but at the end, I was just too tired to keep fighting and too many people could've been negatively affected by a new trial. Therefore, I served my time. That's right, I paid my debt to society by spending five years and a month in Camden County Jail. From there I went to Yardville Youth Correctional Facility, and then to Annadale Medium Security Prison, where I served one month. Around the end of my stay at Annadale, I was transferred out again to a full minimum unit at the Annadale Camp. This was a reintegration unit, and there I was employed as a highway worker by the prison system. That is the facility in which I served out the last eight months of my sentence.

After six years of incarceration, I was finally released on January, 10. Not real sure of what I was going to do with my life, I moved back to South Camden to stay with my mother. I needed to start life over and of course moms was the best place to make a new start. I found a job rather quickly working for a temporary service. In my mind it was going to be just that too, temporary. All I needed was something to help me get back on my feet. Thankfully, after a few months with the temp gig, I found myself a more permanent position working for a landscaping company. Due to being a dedicated and reliable worker, I quickly made my way up through the ranks. My boss showed his approval of my work ethic, and his appreciation for my dedication by trusting me to supervise my own job sites. He gave me the keys to the warehouse that housed all the company's equipment, and I was even authorized to carry blank company checks, which were already signed in order to make business related purchases.

—

During my stay in prison, a long time friend, Denise kept me company. She would write, accept my calls, and even send me money to buy commissary. Denise had been a good friend since before my incarceration, though we had never been intimate. It wasn't long after my release that I started taking a better look at this woman and seeing her in a different light. Her beautiful smile greeted me the day I had been released from prison. I had to concentrate on building myself back up, but she was there from time to time to continue supporting me.

Denise had always been a good friend, and our association together never went beyond that. That's why I was caught by surprise when things intensified between us. Without warning, at least for me anyway, our relationship developed into something that stretched beyond the boundaries of friendship. I gave into our affections for each other without a fight. As the months went by, Denise and her two children became more and more a part of my everyday life. So when the time came for me to move out of my mom's house, it wasn't difficult to decide to invest in a place with Denise. Although, getting a place together would take a little time, we made sure we were together as much as possible.

After a while, her children began to look up to me and depend on me being around. I loved being there for them too; I mean the idea of being a father figure had actually rooted itself in my heart. Fatherhood was definitely something new to me, but it just felt right. I even entertained and maybe day dreamed a little about the idea of marriage. Damn! Who would have ever thought I'd be happy with the, "White Picket Fence" life? I don't know it seemed exciting, but fantasy is always cleared away by reality; and though life started to look very good. Unfortunately, the drama in my world wasn't over, only at the time, I didn't realize it. In fact, my troubles would climax to catastrophic proportions.

February 12, 1997, early that morning, a car sat parked along the curb of a neighborhood street. It was approximately a block up, on the 3000th block of East Camden, an area a drug dealer by the name of Carlos Rosario lay asleep in his bed. According to the police reports, two to four men exited a car dressed in all black. Their faces were covered by full face masks, two armed with a .45 caliber pistol and a .223 caliber military type assault rifle. The plan? To break down the door of Carlos Rosario's house and rob him at gunpoint for any drugs and money he may have had. Police reports say that something went horribly wrong inside the two-story home. When the perpetrators crashed through the door, they weren't quite prepared for what they would encounter.

When he heard the door slam open, Carlos awoke from his sleep. He, too, was armed. When he walked out of his room to the top landing of the stairs on the second floor, he confronted the intruders. Shots rang out; fire was exchanged, and a full blown shootout ensued. Reports reveal that over fifty rounds of ammunition were discharged at the scene.

At Dudley Grange Park, several blocks away, Camden County Park Police Officer, Steven Leoni III, was sitting in his patrol vehicle filling out an incident report for an incident that occurred earlier that night. In his report, Officer Leoni stated, "I heard what sounded like automatic gunfire." Leoni interrupted the writing of his report to go and investigate. He drove his patrol vehicle several blocks in the direction he assumed the gunfire was coming from. He patrolled the area alone, and after he neared the general vicinity, a dark colored car pulled out in front of his vehicle from a side street. The car turned left onto Federal Street, pulling directly in front of Officer Leoni's police cruiser. Without waiting for backup, he took it upon himself to follow the same vehicle he believed held shooters with automatic weapons.

Although Officer Leoni attempted to remain a cautious distance away, the suspects in the dark colored car became spooked at his presence, and while in motion, opened fire on the officer's car. Shots were fired recklessly from the suspects. Leoni never had a chance to return fire; he was pinned down by the oncoming projectiles. The bullets hit the patrol vehicle in the front, shattering the windshield and causing major damage to the engine. One of the projectiles fragmented when it hit the driver's side windshield wiper struck him in the face. He crouched under his dash board and prayed it would provide cover. Seventeen .223 caliber rounds and .45 caliber rounds were recovered by the police at the scene, where Officer Leoni lay waiting on help. Aggravated and angry over the assault of one of their own, the police responded to a report of a dark burgundy Toyota Camry four door sedan found abandoned on a city street. It was several hours later, but it matched the description of the car that earlier obtain the shooting suspect of a cop. When the police arrived and surrounded the car, they found the rear window shattered and shell casings ejected all throughout the back seat.

The Camden Police checked the car's plates in their computer and discovered that the vehicle was registered to a woman by the name of Gloria, which also happened to be my brother's girlfriend. The police called the Pennsauken K-9 unit to come sniff and search the car. The K-9's picked up a scent. Supposedly, the dogs followed the scent trail to a house just a few blocks away from where the car was abandoned. It just so happened to be Gloria's house.

Did the dogs really follow the scent to a house just a few blocks away from the car, or did the police just follow the information provided by their computers? Reports say dogs led them, but who knows? The truth is out there. Either way, the shit was definitely about to hit the fan. Police closed down the entire block and surrounded the house; and to get a clean shot at the suspects, snipers were strategically positioned around the building, just in case the opportunity presented itself. The local authorities were familiar with my brother, and they were aware that the house was his girlfriend's house. The Camden Police Officers wanted Charlie. As far as they were concerned, he had escaped their efforts too many times. Finally, justice would prevail, and they weren't taking any chances. The suspects, whom the police figured were in the house, were wanted for shooting an officer. It was also generally believed that the occupants of the house were armed with automatic weapons, so the police were wary about what they would face inside that house, so they remained cautious.

After the command post was set up around the perimeter, the officers began their attempts at making contact with the people inside the house. They obtained the phone number through their computer records. After several failed attempts to make contact, the police got a break. The quivery voice of a scared young female answered the phone. Police were finally able to confirm what they already knew. Gloria, Charlie's girlfriend owned the house. Erica, Gloria's teenage daughter identified herself and verified that it was only herself and a school friend that had been visiting currently there.

Still suspicious and cautious, police ordered Erica and her girlfriend to exit the home with their hands raised. After several minutes, the girls emerged from the front door with their hands held high. Frightened half to death, they were completely unaware of the situation or why this was happening.

Gloria's daughter was questioned and again told authorities that she and her friend were the only two inside. However, officials were not taking any chances. Before risking a flesh and blood officer, the police sent a remote controlled robot into the house. The Mark Andros 5 was fully mobile with track wheels that resembled those of a tank. It was equipped with cameras to survey whatever area it was searching. The Mark Andros 5 was a sure way to secure the area without needlessly putting their officers at risk, or at least minimized the risk.

After a preliminary search, using the images sent back to the command post from the robot's cameras, authorities determined that the house was safe enough for a full breach. A tactical unit entered the house and further secured the premises. Once the dust settled around the house and authorities were satisfied that they were not going to find anybody there, they automatically assumed my brother had to be their main suspect in the attempted robbery of Carlos Rosario, and the attempted murder of Officer Steven Leoni. With their insatiable animosity towards my brother for "slipping through their fingers twice," a city wide man hunt for Charlie ensued. But Charlie was already aware of the dangers and complexities of the situation, and he was nowhere to be found. Frankly, it was almost as if he had fallen off the face of the earth, yet things got more interesting as time moved on.

Needless to say, when I learned of the situation, I was concerned for my brother. I wanted more than anything for him to be alright, but there really wasn't anything I could do to help him. Charlie was on fire. The authorities were buzzing around hard like a hornets' nest that had just been stirred up. I tried to go on and live my life as normal as possible, but with my brother being named as a major suspect in the shooting of a police officer, I found myself taking on much of the police departments frustration regarding Charlie's absence.

My day to day routines began to be interrupted by regular police harassment. I couldn't drive three blocks away from my mom's house without being pulled over. I don't believe that they were trying to be discreet about it either. They attached themselves to my ass like the tail on a dog, and everywhere I went they followed. Since I was recently released on parole, it was easy for the authorities to keep tabs on me. Even my parole officer joined in on the festivities.

During a routine scheduled meeting, the dirty bitch actually trapped me in her office. Shortly after I arrived to report in, five more parole officers, working in the main building followed me in. They blocked my path to the door, ensuring I had no way to escape. There was really no reason for me to try to escape. Yet, I was tense and nervous as hell, due to being completely trapped. I had no choice but to feel infringed upon when my parole officer cuffed me for no reason. I was stuck, shocked, and confused because I really didn't know what was happening. Was I somehow in violation? Was I under arrest? No one wanted to say anything to me. With my hands still cuffed behind my back, I was moved to the Chief Parole Officers office, and then made to sit in a chair right in front of the Big Boss's desk. After several excruciating minutes, a Camden County Detective and an Assistant District Attorney entered into the room.

With a stern look of agitation on his face, the A.D.A. started talking to the Chief Parole Officer.

"Is this man under arrest?"

"No sir. He's not," the Chief Parole Officer replied.

"Well, since he's not officially under arrest, uncuff him," the A.D.A. ordered.

Following instructions, the Chief Parole Officer removed the cuffs from my wrists. He didn't look too pleased with me; it was as if it was my fault that the A.D.A. had bitten his head off. But I wasn't blind, it was all a ruse. The Camden County Detective and the A.D.A. only wanted to "make nice" with me. It was the good cop bad cop routine.

"Joe," the detective said, "have you heard anything from your brother?"

"No," I replied. "I haven't seen or heard anything from him since all this shit scared him underground."

"Charlie's going down. Period! Eventually, a window will open and we'll get him." The prosecutor stated with eyes hard and filled with hatred.

Still playing the game, the detective gave the A.D. A. a reproachful look. In a more friendly tone of voice, he started talking to me.

"What my friend here means, Joe, is that it really would be better off for everyone if Charlie turned himself in. This thing is big, Joe. And there's a shoot on sight warrant on him. I don't want to see him get hurt."

I wasn't buying their good cop, bad cop routine. I could see right through the act. Still, I did speak the truth.

"I already told you. I haven't seen my brother. I can't do anything to help you or him. Besides, I doubt that he'd want to even talk to me right now. If I do get a chance to talk to him, I'll see what I can do."

I knew my brother well, and I knew how he operated. It was close to impossible to find him if he didn't want to be found. But I threw the cops a bone. Truth of the matter was they didn't want to help Charlie. He was accused of shooting a cop. They wanted to crucify him. I could never be a part of that, but hey, I had to get rid of them somehow. Finally, the good cop needed to say more.

"Okay Joe. If that's how you want to play it, cool. I'm not going to sweat you, but I'm telling you this; this thing is not going to go away. For your brother's sake, I really hope he makes the right decision."

The Assistant District Attorney and the detective didn't even bother to say their goodbyes. They just turned and walked out of the office and left me sitting there alone in the Chief Parole Officer's office. My mind was racing and my thoughts were borderline incoherent, because of the anxiety. They believed that I was hiding something and that I did, in fact, have contact with Charlie. Truth is, I really didn't have any idea where my brother was. I had different reasons than the police did for wanting to hear from Charlie, but yet and still, I wanted to hear his voice. I was worried and wanted to know if my brother was okay.

After leaving the office, I knew the police would be watching me. They were hoping to use me to get to Charlie. They figured if they stayed close, eventually I would lead them to him. I had no choice but to live life as if all was alright. But I knew they were around. I couldn't always see them, but I could feel them. As time went on, undercover agents started to become pretty obvious around the neighborhood. How they figured they would be able to blend in with the community was beyond me. Call it arrogance, but the people in the South Camden area could see right through the facade. Their clean cut looks and healthy faces betrayed them.

Some people in this world delude themselves to the foolish notion that those who are under privileged, also lack intelligence. As one of those under privileged people, I'm pleased to be the one to burst their bubble. People, whether they are rich or poor have an uncanny way of displaying their intelligence, according to their environment. The neighborhood dwellers who have survived their entire lives in the rough streets of South Camden were well in tuned with their surroundings. Undercover cops carry a sour note when they try to hide in the music of the streets.

People who knew me and my family would approach me in the streets to tell me about a couple of guys who'd been sitting in cars, a block away from my mother's house. They'd say, "There's a black guy and a white guy sitting in a car up the block. They just don't feel right." We knew the cops were around. As a matter a fact, everyone in the neighborhood knew. From time to time I even forced them to expose themselves. I just couldn't seem to help myself. One of my most memorable incidents was with a white lady. Checking my rearview mirror had become habitual, so one day as I was driving through South Camden, I noticed a blue Mustang behind me. At first, I couldn't tell whether or not I was just being paranoid. I felt weird about the car. Since I wasn't totally sure, I decided to test my suspicions. I turned off the road I was driving on, randomly changing direction. I watched in my rearview mirror to see how the driver of the Mustang would react. She turned off with me.

Okay, just a coincidence. South Camden is a big place; she could've been heading anywhere. I decided to try again and made another random turn. The white lady driving the blue Mustang turned again in my direction. Alright mother fucker, I thought to myself. I figured, what the hell, they really can't do anything to me anyway. I haven't committed any crimes; so I had a little fun with her. I drove towards the highway with my tail following me the entire way. She didn't realize I was on to her, so when I reached the freeway's on ramp, she was surprised when I made my move. I hit the ramp, driving in the wrong direction. That right! I went up the off ramp, driving against traffic. The Mustang followed. When I reached the top of the off ramp, I pulled onto the highway, falling in sync with traffic and floored it. Free-ballin on the highway, I pushed my 1983 Z-28 Camaro passed speeds of 100 miles per hour. Within minutes, I lost my tail in traffic, and kept driving until I reached my next destination.

When I finally arrived back at my mother's house later that evening, my neighbor, who had been sitting out on his porch all day, had some news for me.

"The fuzz been drivin' by all day."

"Oh yeah," I said.

"Yup. They're parked up the block, too."

"Thanks, man." I nodded, entering the house.

I was so hungry from all that excitement, I walked straight into the kitchen and ate some dinner. Afterwards, I kicked off my shoes and sat on my mom's couch in front of the T.V. It was time to relax. I never bothered to tell her about all the surveillance the cops had around our house. I figured with Charlie being a fugitive, and wanted by the Feds, poor ole' mom had enough stress to deal with that she didn't need to be bothered with anymore worries.

That evening, around eight o'clock, my mom asked me to go to the corner store to pick up some milk. It was just around the corner from our house, so I chose to walk. Mom's place was in the middle of Mt. Vernon Street. When I stepped out of the house, I looked to my left, and then to my right, checking up and down the block to see if I could find something out of the ordinary. I stepped off the porch and walked down towards where Mt. Vernon and Third Street connected. It was away from the direction of the store, but, I wanted to see who was hanging around.

At the corner where the two streets meet, I noticed something a bit amiss in the neighborhood. Across Third Street, where the Board of Education building stood, I could see a car along the curb, facing the wrong direction. It was parked on the street, and had a direct line of sight to my mother's house. Okay, I thought to myself, I see you.

I figured since they wanted to watch me so bad, the least I could do was return the favor and keep my eye on them whenever possible. I turned back to walk up to Mt. Vernon and headed back in the direction of the store I was initially going to go to. When I reached Fourth Street, I was at the top of my block, so I continued on towards Chestnut Street. Suddenly, I noticed a black four door 4x4 Chevy Blazer with dark tinted windows parked along the curb. When I walked by the truck, the passenger door opened. Out of nowhere a white guy with a stocky build sat staring at me. His shoulders were noticeably broader than normal, due to the body armor he wore. Wedged in his hand was the automatic pistol, which he was tightly holding. Finally, he spoke.

"Hey, Joe! Come here for a moment."

Cautiously, I stepped closer to the opened door. I could see three more people. The street lamp glowed faintly on the driver and the passenger; and I could see shadowy figures of two people in the back seat.

"Where's Charlie," the officer asked. It seemed more like a demand than a question.

I was actually worried that they were there to raid my mother's house, so I told the cop my thoughts.

"Look. I don't know. But before you go crazy and get all Rambo on us and shit, I'll take you down to the house myself. That way, you can search each room for yourself. You don't need a warrant. I'll escort you. I just don't need you people kicking down my mom's door, or giving her a damn heart attack. She's already a nervous wreck."

"Nah... We believe you when you say Charlie's not in the house," the cop said. "But you are aware of the fact that there is an S.O.S. warrant out on him, aren't you? That means we can Shoot on Sight." With an air of menace, the officer finished. "Man, we know he's got guns. But we've got guns too. Joe, he'd be much better off turning himself in."

I stood there with a blank look on my face. I nodded my head in acknowledgment. None of the other officers ever spoke, and without additional words, the officer closed the truck door. I eased away and left the cops in their truck as I walked across the street and entered the store. When I came out, they were gone.

Now here's a funny thing. I have been friends with two brothers for quite some time. Joe and Charlie, absolutely no relation to me and my brother what-so-ever, lived on Fifth and Cherry Street, only a couple blocks away from my mother's place. They were like our two alter egos. I got together with them on a regular basis. The irony of our names had hardly ever been lost upon any of us.

A week after my encounter with the cops in the Blazer, I was hanging out on the porch at Joe and Charlie's house. We had been kicking it and shooting the breeze. While talking it up, we noticed a caravan of state police cruisers speeding towards a designated target. We knew that somebody was in for it. Naturally curious, we followed the commotion and walked up the block to see what we could see. I never put two and two together, but I should have. When we reached the end of Joe's block, we could see close to about twenty or thirty squad cars surrounding my mom's house.

"Those faggot ass muthafuckas hit my mom's house," I said. I was pissed, but I was also spooked out of my mind. "Joe. I'ma lay low at your place tonight. Is that alright?" I asked.

"Yeah man, that's cool," Charlie answered, as Joe nodded his head in agreement.

"Shit," Joe said. "We're going to get the car and cruise down the block to get a better look. See what's happening. Wanna come?"

"Hell no, man. I ain't goin' nowhere near that shit down there."

We walked back to Joe and Charlie's house. I went inside to stay out of sight. They went off to observe the raiding of my mom's house. I was worried sick about my mom. I knew she was bugging out; there was no doubt about that, but I had no intentions of showing my face around those cops. I may not have been the object of their frustrations, but if there's one thing I know from growing up in a tough

neighborhood, it's that amped up cops don't always practice the greatest self restraint. When they're zoned out on
something, sometimes they get ugly. And I was the next
best thing to what they hated the most at that moment, my
brother Charlie.

When things finally calmed down and the cops cleared
out, I hurried to my mother's house. A couple of hours had
passed, but I was sure my mom was stressed. I knew they
weren't going to find Charlie, he wasn't there, but when I
arrived, my poor mom was a wreck. She was freaked out and
beyond upset. When I asked her what happened, she told me
that my brother-in-law, Nelson, had just gotten home. Just
as he was about to put his key in the door, the police just so
happened to pull up at the right moment. They rushed him
and roughed him up pretty good, then using his key, they
entered the house.

My mom's house was well fortified. We lived in a bad
neighborhood and had taken sufficient security measures to
keep the bad elements out of our home. All of the accessible
windows were secured with bars. There was a pretty ornery
mutt that patrolled the fenced in part of our yard. The front
door had reinforced steel frames and another security door
with bars, and there was a heavy duty bolt lock on the gate
and two more bolt locks on the entry door. No one was
getting into our house uninvited. The police were aware of
that tiny detail. Unfortunately for my brother-in-law, he just
happened to be in the right place at the wrong time. They
"detained" Nelson and stormed the house with their guns
drawn. They were looking for Charlie; yet all they found
was an old woman and my sister Carmen, Nelson's wife.

As if raiding an old woman's house wasn't enough, the
police had the nerve to use my sister as a damn human
shield. They were so intimidated by my brother and what

he might do, that the officers in the unit followed my sister throughout the house. From door to door, they held my sister in front of them, making her open every door. She was between them and any harm that may have transpired, while the police coward behind her. These people were equipped with helmets, body armor and shields. They were trained professionals. Yet, they still deliberately endangered the life of an innocent civilian. Being Charlie's sister does not make her a criminal. It was all for nothing.

My brother Charlie was nowhere to be found. After coming up empty handed, the police gathered up their equipment and just left as if nothing ever happened. I guess it never occurred to them that Charlie would not have been stupid enough to stay at mom's house just to bring all that heat on her like that. Or they just didn't care. Maybe they just wanted to rattle my brother's cage by rattling up mom.

The raid that took place that day hadn't been executed by the same branch of officers that I'd met in the black Blazer a week before. This was the state police, and their irresponsibility left us angry and bitter. There was no need for such a grand show of force. I was listed as a parolee who had taken residence in my mom's house. While on parole, I personally had no constitutional right to privacy. Although their range of scope would have been limited to my space and belongings, they could have entered the house without a warrant simply because I lived there. All they had to do was come to the house and say, "Hey, we want to search the premises." My mom would have fully cooperated just to keep things peaceful.

Any prior request before that day to search the house was always granted. We didn't have anything to hide. We really didn't know where Charlie was. What we did know was that he wasn't at the house, and we were always willing to reassure the authorities of the fact that we were not harboring fugitives. Later, we learned that Carmen and her mother, both long time friends of the family, also had their houses raided at the exact same time as ours. Three houses in one sweep. It had all been a coordinated effort only to come up with nothing.

After that incident, the authorities gave up on my mom's house, but the damage was already done. Witnessing the extent of their aggression, none of us had any intentions on assisting them by having Charlie turn himself in. It was official. It was us against them, and Charlie was much safer hiding out than he was showing himself.

So much had taken place just two weeks after the shooting of Officer Leoni. The raids had stopped, but I was still being followed around. I wasn't going to let them find Charlie through me. I was worried about my brother, but my hands were tied. There was nothing that I could do for him. I had no choice, but to move on with my life.

I had been anticipating on buying my own home. Since I was living with my mother, I couldn't really go anywhere else because of my parole. Fortunately, a new parole officer was assigned to my case. I didn't know what happened to my other one, but good riddance to her; she made my life as miserable as she could. All I knew was the hateful demon who set me up for the Camden Detective and A.D.A. was gone; therefore, I seriously didn't care why she was replaced. It didn't matter, my new parole officer was so much better. Her whole persona was different, and she actually wanted to see me do well.

She approved of me moving to my own place, so sometime around the end of February, Denise and I finalized arrangements to purchase our own house. In May, we officially moved in. The drama with my brother had really weighed heavily on my mind. The purchase of a new house was definitely a good distraction from all the chaos with Charlie.

The house was on the market pretty cheap. It was only a ten thousand dollar run down row home. It needed work, but Denise, the kids and I, made it our own little project. That made it all the more special. All in all, life was looking up for me.

Unfortunately, even though months had passed since the shooting of Officer Leoni, I still had my tag-alongs. They were good about being where I went. None of it really mattered though. I always knew they were going to be there.

July 19, 1997, Woodlyn New Jersey

At approximately 10A.M. this morning, the Corestates Bank on the corner of Mt. Ephram Avenue and Fairview Avenue was robbed at gun point. Victims of the robbery said that three to four men wearing black clothing with face masks and rifle type guns burst into the bank and ordered everyone to get down on the floor. Witnesses say that the suspects assaulted them to establish control. They said that the robbers timed themselves, and after the victims inside heard someone say, "Times up!" the suspects fled the bank with an undisclosed amount of cash.

Associated Press. September 20, 1997, America's most famous crime show broadcasted a segment of their popular show to seek help from the general public regarding the location of my brother Charlie. It was the first of three shows to be aired on him. Almost seven months had passed since the shooting of the officer and most of the energy around town was dying out. With the broadcast of the crime show depicting Charlie as some crazed lunatic, the media was able to re-spark the dying flame. And the streets were hype again.

The show aired a re-enactment of what supposedly happened the night Carlos Rosario was robbed. It also featured the attempted murder of Officer Leoni III. The segment was actually filmed in North Camden, just miles away from the cruddy streets where it all actually happened. Obviously, I took the time to watch the show.

Ladies and gentlemen, here is where shit really starts to get laid on thick. Anyone with half a brain knows that television never really gets it quite right. Apparently, the crime show was no exception. The producers really twisted the details to arouse the public's anger and gain their sympathy. A word to the wise, whenever you see the words, "Dramatization," please believe that what you are witnessing has been dramatically altered from the true details. The show falsified several facts concerning the incident with Officer Leoni; facts that I was aware of simply because I read the police reports.

According to the show, my brother Charlie planned a hit on a "rival drug dealer". Interesting to me how they used the words, "rival drug dealer" when my brother never really had much interest in selling drugs. They portrayed Charlie as some kind of psychotic lunatic. They dubbed him, "Crazy Charlie" and made him seem as if he was just a raving nut. The information passed on to the public was very inaccurate in many ways. The show claims that Charlie burst into Carlos Rosario's house with an Uzi automatic weapon. The actual police report shows that the shell casings found at the scene were to a .45 caliber pistol and an AR-15 military type assault rifle. No mention was ever made of an Uzi being used.

The producers of the show also claimed that Carlos Rosario confronted the intruders on the first floor of his home and engaged in a fire fight, using an AK-47. The police reports revealed that Carlos was asleep in his bedroom on the second floor, when the suspects entered his place. From the top of his steps on the second floor landing, Rosario fired a .45 caliber pistol, not a machine gun. Ballistics showed that the trajectory of the projectiles fired from the weapons used inside Rosario's home were at angles. Shots were fired from the first floor, aimed at the second floor by the intruders.

While I was watching the show, I saw how the producers described one of the suspects who had been shot in the hand. In the well orchestrated act, the injured suspect sustained a severe wound that bled profusely. Police reports do confirm that a suspect was injured. Fortunately for the suspect, there was little blood and the wound was more like a scratch, which is just another example of how television is made for entertainment.

Because of the unexpected shootout, the intruders were forced to flee Rosario's house. They ran from the house and piled into their Burgundy colored Toyota Camry. The suspects peeled off anxious to get away from the area. They knew someone heard the shots fired, and the police would be on their way. In his police report, Officer Leoni can be quoted as saying, "I was sitting in Dudley Grange Park, writing up on my last arrest, when I heard automatic gunfire coming from the east side of Camden. I put the vehicle in drive and drove to the area which I thought the gun fire might be coming from."

Personally, I'm a bit confused. Is it not procedure for a lone officer to call for back up in a situation where "automatic gunfire" is heard? If not, then it should be. Perhaps Officer Leoni was a bit premature to go and try to investigate something like that on his own. Foolhardy as it may have been, let it be known that we do thank our fine men and women in law enforcement for the risks and sacrifices they make on behalf of the community; especially when those officers wear their badges honorably.

Mr. Leoni went on to say that he was on Federal Street, "at which time I saw a set of head lights coming at me. The suspects observed my patrol vehicle and made a left on Thirtieth Street" From there the show gets kind of silly. They show the officer's patrol vehicle in pursuit of the suspect's car. According to the crime show, a gunman was hanging out of the passenger's window with an Uzi 9 m.m combine. He was firing at the officer from close range. The two vehicles were bumper to bumper as the assailant riddled the officer's patrol car with bullets. In the police reports, the gunman shot out the rear window of the car and fired at the officer from the back seat. Never once did he actually stick his head out the window in the police reports. The spent shell casings and the shattered rear window of the abandoned car were evidence to that.

The biggest falsehood perpetrated by the crime show was their rendition of the close range shooting. The vehicles were never close to each other. The police reports show that the vehicles were so far apart, Officer Leoni couldn't identify the car that he was chasing. As an added shock factor, the crime show's producers showed that Officer Leoni's patrol vehicle stalled out and slow rolled to a stop. The suspects stopped their car as well, only several feet away from Leoni's vehicle. The gunman stepped out of his car, and standing broadside to the officer's vehicle, he unloaded his automatic weapon into the officer's truck. All the while shouting vehemently, "Don't mess with Charlie Rodriguez."

I couldn't believe it. They had actually taken their show to such a low to have the assailant name himself while shooting at the police officer. Please keep in mind that at the time of the filming of the segment, Charlie was not found guilty by a jury or in any other fashion. The producers of the show just threw his name out there on the hear say statement of a tainted source.

The authorities had nothing to actually link Charlie to the crime and the show certainly didn't have anything to substantially show that he committed any of those acts portrayed in their program. In the American justice system a person is supposed to be "Innocent until proven guilty", yet Charlie hadn't been proven guilty of anything, and the American crime show slapped his name on an actor portraying a suspect

The portrayal of my brother on television was flat out ludicrous. It was empty speculation. An informant had given Charlie's name, but he turned out to be an unreliable source. Without any solid information on the facts, they slandered my brother with lies all through the media. So why didn't Charlie just turn himself in and vindicate himself; especially if he was actually innocent? The fact is that Charlie was already on our public servants' shit list. Neither one of us were angels, and the Camden County Police never liked him. Furthermore, he was accused of shooting a police officer, and with an S.O.S. warrant on his head, police had the green light to shoot first and put the pieces together later. The boys in blue had a personal score to settle. Charlie was a perfect candidate for justifiable homicide.

Charlie would've turned himself in, but he truly feared for his own safety. The public doesn't really understand, or care to know the inner politics of the, "streets versus police" world. We do. Police are quick to put a suspect in a box, and Charlie just wasn't willing to risk putting his trust in the police by surrendering. Running may have compounded the potential for danger, but fear can have an adverse effect on one's thinking when his or her life is hanging in the balance.

Chapter 10

On the morning of May 23, 1998, gun shots rang out as three men, all dressed in black, shot their way through the front doors of the Commerce Bank on Marter Ave in Moorestown N.J.

The men all donned masks covering their faces, witnesses said. The employees of the bank stated that they were all pushed into the back area and ordered to the ground. As the robbers made their way out of the bank, they were confronted with car trouble. An employee of the bank was just arriving to work when she was ordered to lie on the ground at gun point by a man wearing a mask. He demanded that she give him the keys to her car.

The bank employee complied with this demand, and the bank robbers escaped, in her vehicle.

CHAPTER 11

Eighteen months had passed since Charlie underground. Rumors spread, claiming that he was Philadelphia and even Puerto Rico. Honestly, I didn't know where Charlie was hiding. I was concerned about him, but all I could do was try and keep the pieces of my own life together. Only I didn't realize how rocky life was about to become.

August 3, 1998, I received a visit from a family member who I had not seen in years. It just so happened that I was at mom's house when my cousin, Fernando Flores, came knocking at the door. As kids, Fernando and I used to hang tough together. As happens to so many childhood friends and relatives, the more the years went by, the more we grew apart. Our lives had taken us down different roads. Most of our contact together over the years had been reduced to family gatherings. I hadn't seen Fernando in ten years before that day. Somehow, within that time, he had become a police officer for the Merchantville Police Department in New Jersey. Police officer or not, Fernando was far from innocent. By the end of his career in law enforcement, he had numerous complaints lodged against him and he found himself as a suspect in an internal investigation at his precinct.

Although Fernando had been closely scrutinized, officials were only able to pin him with possession of a stolen gun. The gun had gone missing from the police evidence locker. His superiors had given him a choice. Be prosecuted, or resign from the force. Disgraced and exiled by his brothers in blue, Fernando walked away from the situation as a regular citizen.

The day Fernando arrived at my mother's house; it was a bit of a surprise. We hadn't seen each other for years and not once had he bothered to contact me during my incarceration. Still, he was my first cousin, his father was my uncle. Even estranged family members popping up for surprise visits aren't out of the ordinary. My sister, Carmen was the one who answered the door that day, and a few moments later, I heard her yelling.

"Joe, Fernando's here to see you!" disappeared sighted in "Fernando? Fernando who?" I yelled back from the other room.

"Our cousin. Fernando Flores."

I'd almost forgotten who the man was. When I walked to the front door and stepped outside to greet him on the porch.

"What'z up cuz? It's been awhile," I smiled, shaking his hand. "Yeah, I know. I wanted to come and offer my support to the family. I know things must be stressful and frustrating with everything that's happened with Charlie."

"Hell man. That shit went down over a year ago."

"I know," Fernando said. "But I've been dealing with my own drama." He lowered his voice. "Can we, uh, talk somewhere?"

"Yea, let's walk down to the corner." We walked away from the house. When we reached the end of the street, I stopped. "What's up?"

"I really need to talk to Charlie myself," Fernando said. "I think I can help him."

It struck me as odd how direct Fernando was when speaking of Charlie. The two of them did have more contact with each other over the years than us. They did keep in touch, and their relationship was somewhat on a different level I guess. Me personally, I just faded away from Fernando, but not for any particular reason. So when Fernando expressed his concerns about Charlie, I didn't read too much into it. He just wanted to help his cousin. I couldn't blame him for that

"How can you help Charlie?" I curiously asked.

"I need to speak to him, Joe," Fernando said.

"Cuz, I can't help you there," I frowned. "I don't even know where the

hell he's at. And I ain't heard from him since all this shit went down." When I confirmed that I didn't know of Charlie's whereabouts, I felt like I'd made myself clear, but Fernando didn't seem to see it that way. He was persistent.

"You gotta find a way to get to him," he insisted. "It's important." I regarded Fernando in silence for a moment. I was thinking to myself, How can this guy help my brother? Finally I spoke.

"I ain't making any promises, but I'll see what I can do." "Alright," Fernando said. "I'll get back to you later."

I walked Fernando back towards my mom's house, following him to a white Ford Mustang that was parked alongside the curb. When he got into the car, we said our good-byes, and I watched as he drove away. I couldn't help thinking to myself that I didn't know where Charlie was, but if Fernando could really help him, then maybe it would be a good idea to try to find a way to get in contact with him. I knew that Charlie could use all the help he could get.

Later that night, I put word out on the streets that I needed to speak to my brother. It was a long shot; Charlie had been out of sight for awhile. He could've been anywhere, but maybe, just maybe, he would get the message sooner or later. A few days later, on August 7, 1998, Fernando again graced me with a visit. This time he showed up at my house, where Denise and I lived with the kids. He never did come to the door. He just honked his horn from the street to get my attention. I walked outside to meet him at his parked car.

"Hey, Joe. What's up," he said, calling me from the driver's side. I leaned into his window to reply .

"Not much. To what do I owe this fine visit? What's up with ya, man?"

"I was just checking in to see if you heard anything yet."

"Damn man! It's only been a couple of days since we talked. I did send word out on the streets, hoping he might get wind of my message. For all I know Charlie is in another country somewhere. You're gonna just have to be patient."

"Okay," Fernando said, handing me a piece of paper. "Here, check this out." I grabbed the paper from his hand.

"What is it?"

"It's a list of frequency numbers," Fernando said. "I just figured Charlie could use them to keep tabs on what the Camden County Cops are up to. If, you can get through to him."

I looked briefly at the numbers on the paper. That was pretty heavy. Police frequency numbers? That's no easy task. I wondered how he got them, but I figured he still had his hookups with his old police buddies.

"Well, thanks. If I hear from Charlie, I'll definitely be sure to give the numbers to him."

A few more subtle pleasantries passed between us, and then Fernando pulled away. I thought to myself that the frequency numbers could really help, but I doubted I'd hear back from Charlie anytime soon. I placed the numbers in my pockets and walked back into the house.

Surprisingly, Fernando showed up at my house again the very next day. He was starting to make a habit of popping up unannounced. He was obsessing about Charlie.

"Fernando, chill the hell out. Nothing's going to change overnight. As soon as I know something, you'll know something." Not that he had much choice in the matter, but he acted satisfied with what I said. "Give me your number, and I'll contact you when I know something." Before leaving, we exchanged phone numbers and then he left.

On August 9, 1998, Fernando pulled up in his Mustang and parked in front of my house again. I was starting to get frustrated with this guy. Why the hell does he keep showing up at my house? When I met him outside, he was still sitting in the driver's seat of his Mustang, so I approached his window.

"Damn, Fernando. What is this, the fourth or fifth time you've popped up at my house in the past week or so? What's up, Fernando, don't you have any friends or something?"

"Sure I got friends." Fernando said.

"Then what's up? I still ain't heard nothin' yet from Charlie. I already told you, I'll let you know something when I do. If I do."

"I know. I know," Fernando said. "But I'm not here to ask about Charlie this time."

"Well that's a switch. What's up then."

"I wanted to see if you'd be interested in buying a gun," Fernando said. "I know how much you like guns and brought over a 9 m.m. and .40 cal. pistol in case you wanted something new."

"Look," I said. "I ain't interested in being around any guns right now, man. I'm on fucking parole. I don't need that shit in my life. It's bad enough I'm trying to get in touch with Charlie. Even though I would like to know how he's doing, I could violate just for having contact with him. Besides, the cops are watching me. And all I really want to do is try to build something with my girl and the lads. I don't want to jeopardize that. I'd appreciate it if you don't try to pull me into shit that could screw things up for me."

"Alright, man," Fernando said. "I didn't mean nothin' by it. I just thought you'd be interested, that's all."

"That's cool," I said. "But now you know."

Fernando was starting to give me bad vibes. After he pulled away from my house, I watched the tail lights of his car fade away, yet again, I thought to myself, Damn I hope this doesn't go bad.

To my surprise, it didn't take as long as I thought it would to hear back from Charlie. Less than two weeks passed, and on August 11, 1998, I pulled in front of my house in my Z-28 Camaro after work. When I stepped out of my car, I noticed a man sitting on the front steps of the house, adjacent to mine on the right. The house had been unoccupied, maybe even abandoned since Denise and I moved into our home with the kids. Seeing the man sitting on those steps put me on alert.

The man's eyes were on me, and they followed me as I stepped out of the car. I could feel his hard stare, as I walked up to the door of my home. Curious as much as I was suspicious, I couldn't help but feel as though the man looked familiar for some reason. The more I thought about it, I realized that he was someone that I recognized around the neighborhood. I had not known the man personally, but his face was familiar.

"Let me talk to you," he called out to me. Cautiously, I made my way over to the steps where the man was sitting.

"Where do I know you from?" I asked. Avoiding my question completely, he spoke again.

"Charlie wants to talk to you."

All my questions disappeared at the mention of Charlie's name. I didn't want or need to know anymore about the man. I no longer cared. The man handed me a folded up grocery bag and I accepted it from him. When I opened it, I saw that there was a walkie-talkie radio with a charger. I looked up at the man questioningly.

"Turn it on at 8P.M. tonight." he said.

Without any more words, he turned and walked away. That evening after what seemed like an eternal wait, eight o'clock finally arrived. Filled win anticipation, I turned the walkie-talkie on. For the first time in over a year, I heard my brother's voice. The reception wasn't quite what I expected, and there were no pleasantries or warm greetings from Charlie. His first words were cold and direct.

"What do ya want? Why did ya put word out that you needed to speak with me? Is mom okay? Or is something wrong?" Caught unprepared for his curt tone, I stammered a little.

"Uh, uh, yeah, man. Mom's fine. She's a little stressed out about all the shit that's gone down, but she's okay." Following my brother's example, I decided to get straight to the point. "The reason I needed to talk to you is because Fernando's been coming around a lot lately asking about you. He claims he can help you. What do you want me to do about him?" Charlie's voice crackled over the radio.

"Don't tell Fernando or anyone that you've talked to me. I ain't got nothin' to say to anybody right now anyway. Besides, I'm working with a lawyer. We're trying to put something together so I can turn myself in safely. I definitely can't turn myself in on my own. I'll conveniently end up having some kind of fatal accident. I'd rather play it safe and cover my ass."

"Who can blame ya," I said. "The cops are pretty pissed. You wouldn't believe the shit that's been goin on…"

I spoke with my brother for at least twenty minutes that night. After all the important business was out of the way, we finally enjoyed some pleasantries between one another. It was like a twisted family reunion, it was all good though. Talking to my brother and knowing he was okay made all the difference; being that we were on an open frequency, we had to play "Cloak and Dagger" over the radio. We were careful not to mention names and places. Still it felt good to talk with him.

Charlie wanted to end it all, but he wasn't quite ready to make the commitment and come out into the open just yet. He still had business to attend to with the lawyer he was consulting with. It would come together, he said to me. We promised to be in touch again. Now that first contact had been made, there was no reason to remain strangers. We just had to be cautious at all times. We ended our conversation with traditional goodbyes and terminated the frequency connection. After our discussion, I felt like the weight of the world had been lifted off my shoulders. I didn't realize how tense and stressed I was. When I learned that Charlie was safe after all that time, my muscles unwound like a snake stretching out under the sun. That night, while in bed with Denise, sleep came easy.

The next day, I made it a point to talk to my mom. I knew she was silently going crazy with worry over her son. She could've used some good news. I admitted to her that I had talked with Charlie. I explained that I didn't know where he was, but that he was okay. I never bothered to tell her what form of communication we used either. The less she knew the better. The only thing that was important was that she was relieved to hear some good news about her son. As expected, the news about Charlie didn't go any further. Not even Fernando was told anything. When he pulled up in front of my house uninvited, as always I walked down the steps to greet him at the curb. First thing out of his mouth.

"What's up? Did you hear from Charlie yet?" It had already been established that I wasn't to say anything to Fernando. Therefore, I respected my brother's wishes.

"I ain't heard nothin' yet, and the truth is, I probably won't hear anything." Fernando nodded clearly understanding what I meant. A brief moment later, he was back at it. "Well, I still have those guns I was telling you about if you've changed your mind."

"And I'm still telling you that I don't want to hear anything about any damn guns."

"Okay. If that's how you feel, I'll respect it," Fernando said. "So tell me, what are you doing on Saturday, the fifteenth?"

"I don't know," I said. "Why?"

"My son is having a Baptism coming up. I want you to come."

"This Saturday," I asked.

"Yeah," Fernando said. "It's gonna be at my dad's house."

"Alright, sure," I said. "I'll be there. I always look forward to seeing the family. Your dad's house is only a couple of blocks away. I'll make it."

I stood outside a little longer talking with Fernando through the window of his car. He never bothered to get out of his car each time he showed up. Though, while we talked, I did notice a hand gun tucked away between his seat and the middle consol. I didn't see it at first, but there it was. Fernando had always been known for carrying firearms. That was his M.O.

I guess some things will never change.

After we finished talking, Fernando and I said our goodbyes and I watched as he drove up the block and out of sight. His Mustang was a nice car to be sure. I could see that he put a lot of money into it. Too bad I would be completely sick of it before everything would be all over.

Unexpected visits had become routine for Fernando, and as usual, he arrived at my house again just two days after our last conversation. It was August 14. I started thinking that he had just grown lonely. Maybe he didn't have any other friends after all. Whatever the case, he pulled up out in front of my house and I greeted him outside. Of course, the first thing out of his mouth was whether or not I talked to Charlie.

"The news is all the same. Fernando," I said

"Alright, well, I'm headed to Philly. I'm gonna go see a gun show. It's right there by the airport near the Ramada. Wanna go?"

"Sounds good, man, but I really can't leave the state or be around guns? No thanks. That's a double whammy for parole. I'll have to pass."

"Okay" Fernando said. "Suit yourself."

And just as he came, he left. That Saturday on the fifteenth, I made my appearance at Fernando's dad's house. I ended up arriving about two hours late to the Baptism. Needless to say, I had missed the ceremony. It really didn't seem to bother anybody. By the time I arrived, the people at the Baptism were already feeling good from their pleasure of choice and getting their groove on.

You know how the Latinos do it!

I walked through the party smiling and making my rounds to greet family and friends. It didn't take long to find Fernando, and it didn't take long for him to bring the discussion around to business.

"Let me holla at ya outside," Fernando said.

"Damn, man," I said, "I just got here."

"I know," Fernando said, "just give me a few minutes."

I sighed and reluctantly followed him. He led me through the living room and out the front door. We walked up the sidewalk, passing by houses as we headed towards the corner. When we arrived at the end of the block, and out of ear shot of anybody else, I questioned him.

"Okay Fernando. What's up now?" As if I didn't already know what was coming. Eager to oblige, Fernando replied.

"So, did you hear from him yet?"

"No Fernando. I still haven't heard anything from him yet."

"Oh well I hope you hear something from him soon." Fernando said with a quiet thoughtful look on his face, almost as if he was genuinely disappointed. "On another note," he said, "I just sold six guns." He pulled a large roll of bills from his pocket and flashed them in my face. "Joe, I can get any type of gun or accessory from the gun show. I don't even have to show my ID. It's sweet. I pick'em up for low prices and jack'em up on the streets. I'm going back to Philly tomorrow to pick up some more. Do you want to buy some?"

"Nah, man. I'm good. I've already told you I'm not really interested in any of that shit right now. Besides, I can't be spending money all recklessly on some crazy shit. I'm more concerned with saving money, so Denise and I can get our house in order. It's an old house and it needs a lot of work."

"Okay," Fernando said. "I can respect that. The outside of the house didn't look too bad. I never did see the inside."

"That's because you keep beeping your damn horn outside every time you show up," I said interrupting him.

"True enough," he said. "So you need a little money, huh? Well, tell ya what. If you want, I can lend you three thousand dollars right now."

I was surprised by the offer. I hadn't seen the guy in such a long time, we were just beginning to get reacquainted again, and here he was offering me money. Hell, what's family for? Not even trying to hide my shock, I replied.

"Are you serious? Three grand, just like that?"

"Yeah I'm serious," Fernando said, "we're family ain't we? I can look out for you if I want."

"Wow, cuz," I said, "That's pretty heavy. I could definitely use it, but I won't be able to start paying you back until sometime in the middle of September. Even then I'd only be able to give you a hundred dollars a week'"

"I can work with that," Fernando said.

Fernando handed me the roll of bills. It felt nice in my hands. I mean, who doesn't like the feel of a wad of money in their hands? When I counted it out, there was only twenty-five hundred dollars, not three thousand like he said. But who was complaining? That's still a nice chunk of cash, and it would definitely help me with making progress on the house. With a smile and a thank you, I shook my cousin's hand in appreciation for his contribution.

Little did I know that I had just made a deal with the Devil. Sunday, August 16, 1998, the very next day, Fernando again arrived at my house. It's always good to see family, but a line needs to be drawn somewhere. I was beginning to think this guy was stalking me. When I walked outside to meet him, I had grown frustrated.

"God damn, man. What now? Didn't we just see each other yesterday?" Without responding to my reaction to his visit, he replied. "Come on. Get in. I wanna show you something."

I stood there looking at him for a second. My irritation was quickly forgotten and replaced with curiosity. What did this guy want to show me? I walked around to the passenger side of his Mustang and the minute I sat down and shut the door, we were on our way.

"So where are we going?" I asked.

"I wanna take you to my dad's house." My irritation returned. "I just left your dad's house yesterday. What the fuck, Fernando? Why

do you keep coming around here with stupid shit?"

"This isn't stupid. I told you. I want to show you something.

Something I didn't have a chance to show you yesterday, because of all

the people that were there."

Fernando's father lived in a two-story row home in a slummy area in New Jersey. The neighborhood was pretty run down, but it was home for us. Trash was blowing all over the streets, crack heads were prowling the area, many wandering around like zombies, and drunks were stumbling around or passed out on the side-walks. However, I paid it little attention. That was all regular everyday stuff to us. When we pulled up in front of the South Camden home, I wasn't. Hell, I had just been there the night before.

When we entered my Uncle Ellio's house, I walked through the living room and straight into the kitchen, leaving Fernando behind. The smell of rice and seasoning lingered in the air. Aunt Lucy was cooking something that smelled phenomenal. It definitely stirred up hunger inside me. I walked up to her and gave her a quick kiss on the cheek to announce myself.

"Did you have a good time yesterday?" She asked.

"I sure did. Thanks, Tia." I responded. After showing my respects, I walked back to the living room to find Fernando. He was standing in front of a large China cabinet placed alongside the living room wall. My Uncle Ellio was standing there with him. Fernando stretched his hand out and reached to the top of the cabinet. When he pulled his hand back, he was holding a box about six inches in width and almost two feet in length. It was square and narrow. When Fernando opened it, he revealed a 9 m.m. combine rifle. He reached up to the top of the cabinet again and pulled down his "Bomb Squad" cap, the name of his paint ball team, and placed it on his head. He handed me the rifle with a childlike grin on his face.

"Check it out. Ya like it?"

"Yeah! It's nice." I smiled, admiring the light gray plastic structure of the rifle.

While I inspected the 9 mm combine, Fernando reached up to the top of the cabinet again. This time he pulled down a .45 caliber automatic pistol. I handed him back the combine rifle and replaced it with the .45. It was nice. Smooth black coloring with a comfortable pistol grip, it felt real good in my hand. Too bad I couldn't really indulge in my own interests in guns too much. Parole definitely had me on a tight leash. While I appreciated the craftsmanship of the .45, Fernando stared at me quietly for a moment.

"I got those at the gun show in Philly last night."

"I like 'em, they're nice."

"What's up, then?" Fernando asked, "Do you wanna buy 'em or

what? We can take the serial numbers off and clean them up for you."

My anger threatened to resurface, but I didn't want to make any kind of scene in front of my uncle. I've already explained to Fernando how I felt about being around guns, let alone buying them. Yet, he still persisted in his attempts to get me to buy one. He really did get under my skin with his pushiness, but because I was at my uncle's place, I kept it civil; even though I really did want to strangle the son-of-a-bitch.

"No, Fernando," I said. "I'm not interested in buying anything. Still."

"Alright. Well I'm gonna go back again to get more before the place moves on. Don't be afraid to ask if you change your mind."

"Fine, Fernando. But I doubt it'll become an issue."

CHAPTER 16

Growing up in the same neighborhood your whole life, it's inevitable that you will build lasting relationships with people. Most of the time, people just fade apart and go their own way or grow intolerable towards each other. Others just turn out to be pieces of shit.

Jose Soto and I both grew up in South Jersey. He lived just a block away from my mom's house. We had minimal associations with each other growing up, but as time went by, Jose and I developed a tighter bond. When I was released from prison in 1997, Jose Baez picked me up in his gray Chevy Blazer with Jose Soto riding shot-gun. They both treated me to some strip club entertainment. Once again, Jose Soto and I really started to build our friendship from that point.

Soto and I even ended up working for the same landscaping company. He only lived about six to seven minutes away from where Denise and I had bought our home. In the mornings, I would pick Jose up at his house and we would ride to work together. It was a convenient arrangement, especially since he lived in route to the job's main office. Jose had his own vehicle, but carpooling made it easier on us with expenses. Besides, what are friends for anyway, if you can't rely on them for a ride to work?

When you have friends; you lookout for each other, right. August 18, 1998, I cashed in my favor from Jose. He agreed to meet up with me at my place later that day after work. I needed help moving my double-stacked washer and dryer into the basement. It really didn't take that much effort; it was only one piece of equipment. We carried the thing through the house and down the cellar steps. We set the appliance along the wall where all the connections were and it was ready to be used. After the washer and dryer were set, we decided to walk outside to get some air. We walked over to the opposite side of the street. There was a building that looked like it was some kind of warehouse or something, because around the back there was an open docking area.

The place was accessible through there, for more reasons then one. But Jose and I had other plans. The two of us were both fans of the "Oh so violent" paint-ball sport. There was nothing like pegging each other with little hard rubber/plastic balls filled with colorful paint flying at high velocity. I guess there's just something about the allure of going to war.

After inspecting the rear of the building for entry ways, Jose and I walked back around to the front discussing plans on how to arrange a good day for a paint-ball fight. We were kicking around some ideas on how to set up the inside of the building, so we could shoot each other up when Fernando's white Mustang pulled alongside of us and parked

"What's up, guys? Hey, Joe, I gotta talk to you for a second" Fernando said, getting out of his car. He walked to me and Jose and stood in front of us.

"Well. Here I am, Fernando. What's going on?"

"Is your friend cool," Fernando asked, nodding towards Jose. "Can we talk around him?"

The atmosphere immediately got a little thick around us. I didn't know what Fernando wanted to discuss, but it was obvious that it was pretty heavy. Jose didn't say anything, but I knew him to be a good guy, so I didn't object to anything.

"He's alright, Fernando. Go ahead."

"Okay. I've got something big for us," Fernando said. "I have a friend who works for an armored car company. He's been with the company for awhile and has a good track record with them. He has a bad gambling habit as well and went and got himself in some serious debt. He's desperate and needs a way out from under his bookie. There'll be over a million dollars packed in the back of the truck that he'll be guarding."

"Whoa, whoa, whoa, whoa," I said. "What the hell are you talking about? The truck that he'll be guarding? Why should I care about the truck that this guy will be guarding?" Jose grew noticeably uncomfortable.

"I'm saying we rob it," Fernando said.

"Are you crazy? Rob an armored truck? You must've fell and bumped your head somewhere on your way over here. I can't believe you just said that."

Jose had walked away the moment Fernando spoke the words, "Rob it." He had no intentions on being around for that discussion.

"It'll be a sure thing," Fernando continued on. "It's completely an inside job. It'll be nice and easy and nobody will get hurt. We just need three guys willing to do this thing and they must be capable of pulling it off, and making it look good."

I was shocked that this man could bring something like that to my attention at this period of my life. I was still working on putting the pieces of my own life together and this fool wanted to come to my house and talk some nonsense about robbing an armored truck. Fernando continued talking.

"Truthfully, I think this could be a good hit for Charlie." "What the hell does Charlie have to do with all of this?" "I know he can use the money," Fernando said. "You just have to find

a way to get in contact with him."

I couldn't help but just stare at him like he was an invader from another planet. This guy really knew how to cause ripples in a pond. While I was contemplating Fernando's craziness, I heard the rev of an engine. I looked towards the street and I saw Jose driving away. He left and never said goodbye. Bringing my attention back to Fernando, he spoke.

"What are you doing right now?"

"Nothing now. You just scared my company away."

"Good," Fernando said. "Get in the car and take a ride with me. I

wanna show you something."

This guy was really starting to get under my skin. I had told him time and time again that I had no interest in his crazy ideas. I didn't want any drama in my life, but he couldn't seem to get it through his thick skull. I wanted to tell him to get lost. I didn't care about what he wanted to show me. But he did loan me twenty-five hundred dollars, and in my way of thinking, I was obligated at least to be courteous. My head heavy with weariness I got into his car thinking, that damn deal with the Devil. Once seated inside the car, Fernando started talking again.

"I wanna show you this spot real quick." He pulled away from the curb and when he drove up the block, I questioned him.

"What spot are you talking about, Fernando? And how far is it?"

"The Walt Whitman Services Plaza," Fernando said. "It ain't too far. It's the place where my boy will be with the armored truck if we do this job."

I didn't say anything to Fernando. I already knew I wasn't getting involved in this. Basically, I was just humoring him. At least that's the way I looked at it. So I sat quietly as we drove down route seventy towards the New Jersey turnpike. When we finally arrived at the rest stop, Fernando used the rear service entrance, avoiding any turnpike toll booths. I immediately recognized the area. My landscaping company did work under a Motorola tower right off the property of the service's plaza, on June 30, 1997. A large grass area stretched out behind the building of the rest stop. I had never actually been there or in the parking lot, but it was clearly visible from the location we had worked.

And was very familiar now.

"Fernando, what are you doing here," I said. "You can't be serious." "You're damn right I'm serious," Fernando retorted back. "I really need this. And you really need to find Charlie and get him to help. Looking at Fernando with suspicion, I asked.

"Why is it so important to you that you bring Charlie in on this?"

"Because I know you two are reliable. This is an inside job, man. We can really blow up off this thing. I have it all set up already. All we have to do is follow through with the plan. And I know Charlie could use the money."

As he spoke, we slowly cruised through the rear parking lot. Approaching the front of the building, Fernando began laying out the plan he had concocted.

"There's an ATM machine in that building. My friend's job is to fill the machine up with money. He'll park the truck at the front of the building. When he gets out, he's going to leave the door open. We'll run up on him, secure the truck, and he'll just play it out as it goes. We'll lay him down and get the money. No muss, no fuss. We should come out with over a million dollars to split."

My stomach grew ill. I felt hollow like you do when you finally figure out that Santa Clause isn't real. This guy was a real character. I wasn't interested in any crazy capers. A million dollars sounded tempting, but even that didn't excite me enough to rob an armored truck. I had to get Fernando to understand a simple phrase, I'm not interested." But that task was harder then it seemed. I knew my brother Charlie didn't want to talk to anyone. He preferred to be left alone, but I had to get this jerk to finally get the message. Maybe if Fernando heard the word, "NO" from Charlie's mouth, he would let the whole thing rest or just go bug somebody else with it. As I finished listening to Fernando and his craziness, I had to say something.

"Fernando, just take me home."

"What's up? You don't like the plan?"

"No I don't want..," I was saying before I cut myself off. I was frustrated. But, once I knew I could control myself, I tried again. "Just take me home. We'll talk later."

Looking at me questioningly, but saying no more, Fernando exited the rest stop parking lot and headed back to my house. When we arrived on my block, Fernando parked. I got out of the car and turned to face his passenger window.

"Wait here a minute." I said, walking towards the house. After entering, I shut the door and ran upstairs. I went to my room, grabbed the walkie-talkie that I had stashed away and put it in my front pocket. Overwhelmed, I went back through the front door. When I returned to the Mustang, I got back into the passenger seat.

"Come on. Let's drive."

"Okay," Fernando said, "Where to?"

"Just drive up the block and turn on Seventh Street," I said. "Then hit

Royden." Fernando followed the directions I gave him. "Okay, cross over Broadway and keep going straight." Not too far passed Broadway, I instructed Fernando find an empty space to park along side of the curb.

"What are we doing here?" Fernando asked. Without giving him an answer, I pulled out the radio and turned it on. Into the speaker I spoke.

"Yo, Yo. Come back. Your cousin wants to talk to you."

"What's that for? Who ya callin'?"

I just continued to send my voice out over the air waves, ignoring Fernando, waiting for a response. After a few minutes, a voice finally crackled back.

"Yo. I'm here. What's up?"

"Hey, man," I said, "I got our cousin here. I think you should talk to him." Fernando's expression was one of a pleasant surprise when he heard Charlie's voice. When I handed him the walkie-talkie, the excitement was evident in his voice.

"Yo. What's up, cuz? Damn. How ya been, man?"

"I'm alright Just been chillin' and layin' low. You know. I'm trying to figure this shit out," Charlie's voice answered back.

"Well, I have an idea that just might help you with your situation." Fernando went into explaining his plan for the rest stop robbery. Of course he couldn't be specific over the radio. The frequency was open, and there was no telling who might be listening. Charlie listened quietly, and when Fernando finished, he spoke.

"Sounds good and all, but for real, I'm not really trying to get caught up in anymore bullshit. I've got enough to deal with as it is. I just wanna work with this lawyer and try to get this whole thing settled. Safely! So I gotta tell ya no on this. I'm not interested." Charlie's answer never deterred Fernando. He continued to run his mouth.

"Just think about it. You don't have to answer now, but this could be a great opportunity for you. If everything goes well, you'll have plenty of money to cover your lawyer's fees. Don't decide right now. Sit on it a couple of days and have Joe get back with me later."

I listened to Fernando as he basically begged Charlie to jump on board with the plan. I couldn't help thinking to myself. Why can't this guy just take no for an answer? What the hell is his problem? I already knew what Charlie's thoughts were. I would talk with him one on one later. But at the moment, I just let the scenario unfold like I knew it would. I listened as Fernando begged, and Charlie just simply said no. After the conversation was over, we said our goodbyes and I replaced the radio into my pocket. We pulled away from the curb and headed back to my place. The drive back was quiet. I could see that Fernando was feeling dejected.

Too Bad!

When we arrived back at the house, Fernando had to say something.

"Look, Joe. We could really get paid off this thing. You can buy a nice house in the burbs and get Denise and the kids out of Camden. Give them a better life. Don't walk away from this thing. Give it some thought." Opening the car door, I looked to Fernando.

"You have my answer, and my mind is made up. I'm not interested, and Charlie's not interested. So just let it go. Go find someone else to do it with you." I insisted, stepping out of the car, and immediately walked into my home.

Later that evening, after Fernando was long gone, I got into Denise's car and took a long ride. I drove alone to the water front. There, I found a nice quiet, secluded spot and parked. I tried not to look too conspicuous and when I was comfortable with the scene, I pulled the walkie-talkie out of my pocket.

"Yo, bro. What's up? Come back." Charlie answered instantly. "Yo. What the hell is up with that idiot? Is he stupid or something? I'm out on the run and that asshole wants me to do a robbery with him? He's crazy. The cops are just waiting for a reason to shoot my ass. They'd love for me to do something like that, so it would make it that much easier to put a bullet in my head. What's up with that guy?"

"I don't know," I said. "But he's been on me about it for awhile now. I was hoping that if he heard you say no that he'd leave us alone about it."

"Too many things could go wrong messin' with something like that. It's too much of a risk."

"I agree," I said.

"Besides," Charlie continued, "the cops want me so bad they could be using Fernando to bring me out in the open."

"Do you think Fernando would do something like that," I said.

"Hell yeah. The son-of-a-bitch is a dirty cop. At least, he was a dirty cop. He's the worse kind of person. He has no loyalties and there's no separating right from wrong for him. He's all about himself, no matter who gets fucked in the process. Just tell him we're not interested and leave it at that."

As far as I was concerned, my brother's intentions were clear. This thing wasn't happening. At least not with us involved. That evening the conversation with my brother ran late into the night. I was exhausted and my head was spinning with all the shit that was happening in my life. When I finally walked through the front door of my house, I wasted no time. I went directly to my bedroom and fell asleep.

The next morning when I awoke, I was weary and still tired. It didn't matter. I had to earn money to make a living. I mean, it was clearly obvious that the bills weren't going to pay for themselves. Therefore, I had to get out of my comfortable bed. As I mopped about, I performed my daily ritual; took a piss, washed my hands, face, and brushed my fiery ass mouth. Eventually, I made it out the front door, and left the house the way I would any other morning. As usual, I drove to Jose's house to pick him up for work. There he was standing outside as usual. While cruising down the highway, Jose started talking.

"Yo. What was up with that crazy dude talking that robbery shit, yesterday?"

"That was my cousin Fernando. He's a crooked cop who is now out of a job. He's a little bugged out."

"A cop," Jose said with shock in his voice. "What the hell are you doing talking about a robbery with a cop? Are you nuts?"

"No. I'm not nuts. He's family. Besides, that dude was more crooked than the letter s. He broke the law more as a cop than most people ever do as a civilian."

"Damn," Jose said. "That's some pretty crazy shit. A real crooked cop. Hell, he carries that gun around like he's still a cop."

"Oh, you seen that, huh," I smirked. "I guess he does. He got booted off the force awhile ago, but I suppose he never fully accepted it. He always carries at least one gun around with him."

"My girl's at home pregnant with twins," Jose said. "She'd kill me if she knew that guy was talking like that around me."

"Yeah, tell me about it. Denise would hang me by my nuts. But if it's any consolation for you, I'll testify on your behalf to your girl that you walked away as soon as Fernando mentioned the word, 'robbery'."

"Oh, yeah? Well, I appreciate your bravery, but you should be careful yourself. My girl is liable to hang you by your nuts, if she thought that you let that asshole come around me." We laughed. "But seriously," Jose said, "watch yourself with that guy."

The rest of the ride to work was nothing more than idle chit chat we kept the conversation light and away from any stressful subjects. Unfortunately, I couldn't get Fernando and that whole situation out of my mind. He was in my head, and that worried me. After I returned home from work that evening, I washed up and sat down on my sofa to relax. To anyone who has never worked doing landscaping jobs, it's taxing on your body. I was comfortable and dozing off, when I heard a loud, obnoxious noise coming from outside.

"Joe," Denise hollered out to me, "your cousin's outside beeping his damn horn."

"Damn that guy," I cursed to myself. "It's seven o'clock at night. Don't he know that we have old people for neighbors"

The elderly couple that lived next door were nice people, and respectful. They lived quietly and pretty much kept to themselves. I really didn't want them to think of us as bad neighbors. I hurried outside and headed directly for Fernando's car. When I stepped at his car window, he had this stupid look on his face.

"What the hell is wrong with you?" My face was wrinkled in anger and my voice was hoarse with frustration. "I've got neighbors, Man. Show some damn respect. Don't come here honking your horn all crazy. Just come to the door and knock like any normal person." Fernando completely dismissed my entire show of dissatisfaction.

"My friend's in trouble, Joe. The bookie's threatening to break his legs now. We have to help him." I stood on the sidewalk staring at Fernando with a blank expression on my face.

"What's this 'We have to help him,' shit" I stood on the sidewalk staring at Fernando with a blank expression on my face. Then I couldn't help but speak again. "We have to help him. Man, I ain't gotta help anybody."

"He really needs my help."

"What the hell does any of this have to do with me, Fernando? I don't even know the guy."

"It doesn't really have anything to do with you. But come on, Joe," he pleaded, "you're the only one I can trust. And this is my chance to really help a friend."

"And make a big score," I said sardonically.

"Well, yeah; that, too." Fernando said, feigning innocence. "But we can really do it. I wouldn't bring it to you, if I thought it would be too risky. We hit it, split the money, and just walk off into the sunset."

"Yeah, whatever," I said. "This isn't fucking 'Tequila Sunrise', shit really gets fucked up in the real world. I don't want to hear any more about this shit. Fernando, go home." Fernando's persistence was infuriating.

"Let me talk to Charlie again."

"Hell no," I said. "That's completely out of the question." I knew I should've never let Fernando talk to Charlie. Now he's going to be like a damn stray dog. Feed him once… "Fernando, you already got his answer, and nothing's changed. Stop bothering us about it. God damn, Fernando. Get the message already."

I turned and walked away from the car. I was fed up and I didn't want to hear any more of what he was trying to sell. I never even gave him a chance to respond. The man acted as if he didn't know the definition of the word, 'no'. I disappeared into my house and left Fernando and his craziness out on the curb. Once inside the house, I could see that Denise was concerned by her look and questions.

"Babe? What's up with your cousin? We've been together for awhile now and I've never seen him come around. Now, out of the blue, he's here every day."

"He's alright," I said. "He's just one of those family members that you wish you could toss out with the garbage. But you know how it is. Family is family. He probably doesn't have anyone else to play with right now."

Personally, I was starting to doubt that very assessment myself. I could see the skepticism in Denise's face as well. Out of respect, she didn't comment on it. All she said was, "Shit, if he suffocates others the way he suffocates you, it's no wonder he doesn't have anyone else to play with. He chased them all off."

Denise made light of it, but still the question remained, 'Why was Fernando so persistent with his visits lately?' All of a sudden, I was his only friend, it didn't sit well with me. Still, I convinced her that he was a family member who needed companionship.

CHAPTER 19

August 20, I figured it was my turn to bug Fernando. He worked as a manager for a paint ball store at a flea market in Columbus, New Jersey. Like myself, Fernando was a paint ball fanatic, and he loved to shoot it out. It was time for me to use Fernando's position at the paint ball store for my own gains. What's the point of having a family member in a favorable position if you can't take advantage of it? So I called him.

"Hey, Fernando. It's me, Joe. What's goin' on?"

"I don't know, you tell me. You're the one calling."

"Well, I'm trying to hook up with a good deal on some paint ball gear.

You work for a paint ball shop, I was wondering if you could hook me up with something."

"Yeah, cuz," Fernando said. "I can definitely do something for you. I can get you whatever you need for half of the store price. Shit, I already have a bunch of stuff in the trunk of my car. If you want, I can stop by your house later."

Yeah, I bet you will, I thought to myself, before replying.

"Cool. I'll be here."

Later that evening, Fernando made good on his word. This time when he arrived, he didn't pull up honking his horn like some nut. He acted more civilized and actually came to the door and knocked. When I opened the door, I saw that he was holding a white plastic bag in his hand. I also couldn't help but notice the bulge in his waistline from where he had his gun tucked.

"Is that the gear?" I asked, pointing at the white bag.

"Nah. There's just a bunch of paint balls in this bag. A shit load of them, actually."

"I asked for a mask and other protective gear. What happened to that shit," I said.

"When you called earlier, I wasn't at home. When I checked in the trunk, this was all that I found."

"But you said the gear was in your trunk, when I called."

"Obviously I was wrong." Fernando said. "This is all I've got. But I do have the mask and other shit at my house. I can get it to you later or come to my spot. "

"Okay, well. I guess I don't have much choice in the matter." I looked disappointed, grabbing the bag out of his hand. "Wait here a second. I'll be right back."

With the bag of paint-balls in my hand, I turned and left Fernando standing in the door way. I ran up the stairs to my bedroom. I grabbed my paint-ball gun and ran back down the stairs. When I returned to where Fernando was waiting, I handed him the gun so he could see the make and model.

"Hey, this is a Spyder," Fernando said. "We have these at the shop. We get parts and accessories for it, too. Shit, I can get parts for this bitch at my house. We can hook this puppy up and help make it shoot better."

"For real? That's what I like to hear," I said. "I can go to your place and check it all out when I go get the mask. Instead of you coming back here. But I want to get the mask real soon though. I'm goin' paint-ballin' this weekend with Jose."

"Speaking of Jose," Fernando said. "Where's he at? Where does he live?"

"He ain't here. Why?" I said, looking suspiciously at Fernando.

"I can see he's not here," Fernando said. "But where's he at? I mean, where's he live? Does he stay close by or what?"

"I'm not going to tell you where that man lives," I said. "If he wants you to know where he lives, let him tell you."

"Damn, cuz," Fernando said. "Relax. I was just askin. I don't want to molest the guy or anything. I was just curious. I just asked you because I really don't know the guy to be asking him personal questions like that."

"If you don't think you know him well enough to ask him, maybe you shouldn't be asking me."

"I'm asking because I already told my friend about the three of you."

"The three of who?"

"You, Charlie and Jose," Fernando said. "He knows that I already told all of you about the armored truck robbery.

"Jose doesn't know about anything. You scared him off before you got too far into the plan, remember?"

"True, but he was there when I mentioned it," Fernando said. "At any rate my friend's a little pissed that I let the cat out of the bag and nobody wants to come along for the ride. He'd rather me get you guys to come along instead of telling someone else about the plan and spreading it out there more.

"I really need this, Joe. I know I can trust you and Charlie. The two of you would never sell me out or turn on me. Since Jose already knows about it, and he's your friend, I figured, fuck it, he might as well ride as a fourth man. It's all set. I just need the bodies."

"What the fuck is your problem? Why is it so difficult for you to get it through your thick head that I'm not interested? You know what? It's time for you to go. Every time you show your face you want to talk about this shit. You're really starting to wear out your welcome." I said in a firm voice not hiding my irritation.

"Chill out, Joe," Fernando said. "I don't mean any harm in it. I just want to do something big for us all. You know, make it a family affair."

"That's all fine and well, but I don't need that shit in my life. So take it somewhere else."

"Alright. I'll try to stop bothering you about it. But I really can't think of anyone else who would be better suited for the job. Anyway, are you still gonna come to the apartment to pick up the paint-ball gear?"

"Yeah, Fernando," I said. "I'll come by when I get the chance. It'll be soon though. But you have to drop this nonsense about that robbery."

After Fernando left, I was angry at the idea that this man was so insistent on bursting into my world. I was content with the way my life was going. I had no reason to put it all at risk. My girl was a good girl. Her children were my children, they loved me, and I loved them. Plus, I knew that Charlie was okay. That was good enough for me, or it should've been anyway. When I closed the door, I didn't bother going upstairs. Denise was in our bedroom, while I was talking to Fernando. She knew me better than anyone, and I really didn't want her to see me upset, so I walked into the kitchen and headed straight for the refrigerator. When I opened the door, my favorite beverage was staring me in the face. One hundred percent orange juice; just what I needed.

I took the carton of O.J. out of the ice box and sat at the kitchen table. I pondered over the different events that had taken place in my life. Things were well with the house. We had begun the remodeling process. The twenty-five hundred dollars that Fernando gave me was a good start, but it was just a start. The process was slow, but little by little, it was coming along. Denise and I were getting along well and the kids couldn't be better. Considering everything in my life, I could really say I was at my best at this point and time. Then I started thinking about Fernando and his enthusiasm for pulling off the caper of the year.

I thought of my brother and all that he's been through and the strain his situation has put on our family. Suddenly, a horrible thing happened, the thought of how a million dollars in cash could change everyone in my immediate family's life, crept into my head. Charlie would be able to get himself a good lawyer. I know mom could use some help financially. She was getting up there in age. Hell, even Denise and I could use the extra help with our expenses. Who couldn't?

But it was all just a thought. There couldn't be any justifying taking a risk like that. Could there?

When I finally turned the lights off in the kitchen to stroll upstairs for bed, I was sure to take the paint-ball gun with me. Didn't need any of the 'lil' guys shooting an eye out.

CHAPTER 20

Saturday, August 22, Fernando arrived at my house early that day, stressing me about letting him talk to my brother. I argued with him until I was literally blue in the face, but it did me no good. He eventually drove me crazy and wore me down.

"Let me talk to Charlie, Joe," he begged one additional time. "Jesus Christ, Fernando. I'll get the damn walk-ie-talkie," I said. "Just stop geekin out."

I turned away from his car and walked back into the house. A few minutes later, I returned, got into his vehicle and told him to drive. I gave him directions to where I wanted to go. During the drive, we sat in silence. We really didn't have much to talk about. I didn't care to hear anymore about his idea; and as far as I was concerned, I had made myself clear. Charlie did, too, but this guy just had to hear it again.

So be it.

We arrived at the waterfront, and I told Fernando to find a place to park. I told him to get a good place, out of the way and inconspicuous. When we found a sufficient spot, he pulled off the road and parked I pulled the walkie-talkie out of my pocket and handed it to Fernando.

"Here. You already know not to use any names. Just speak into the speaker. If he's listening, he'll answer." Fernando hesitated for a moment, looking at the radio as if he hadn't understood what I told him. Then he finally spoke.

"Ah, hello? Yo. You there?" Several moments passed before Charlie's voice came crackling through the speaker.

"What's up, now? What ya want?" Fernando didn't even greet Charlie, he just jumped right in.

"Hey Cuz. Hear me out before you jump to any conclusions."

"I thought I already heard you out and said all I needed to say," Charlie said.

"Just hear me out," Fernando said in an earnest voice. "We would be crazy to pass up this opportunity. I mean, it's so sweet. My boy doesn't even know who any of you are. He can only identify me and you ain't got to worry about me."

"Doesn't matter," Charlie said. "The risks are too big with something like that. Someone could get hurt or even killed."

"But how," Fernando pleaded. "It's an inside job. There'll be no resistance, no tripped alarms, nothing. Nobody's gonna get hurt."

"I don't know," Charlie said.

Hearing the doubt in Charlie's voice, Fernando sensed blood and moved in for the kill.

"Everything's all set. If we need to, we can get cars from City Select. I have a connection there. We can have the papers doctored. No links to us. Over a million dollars, cuz. More than any one of us needs. Just imagine the break down on that five ways. That's more than one hundred thousand dollars apiece. That's a minimum. Lawyer fees? Commissary? Man you just name it, and no problem. That money will provide whatever you need to help get you through your situation. Come on, Man. It's my turn to come up. And I could really use your help. We can all come off big on this one."

Inside the car, there was nothing but a pregnant silence. Fernando and I both sat quietly anticipating Charlie's response. I personally couldn't believe that Charlie was actually considering it. After all this time arguing and fighting with Fernando to shut him up about it. Charlie was actually entertaining the idea. He must've been hanging on by his last thread. When Charlie finally answered, his voice burst through the speakers.

"Okay. I'm in."

"Great," Fernando said. He was as ecstatic as a kid in a toy store.

I sighed, disappointed that my brother had actually caved in to Fernando's pressure. I guess Charlie had his own pressure weighing down on his mind. Who was I to judge really? Charlie had to be under a lot of stress and he was desperate for a way out.

"Hey," Charlie said.

"Yeah, I'm here," Fernando said. His voice giddy with excitement. "Come get me at Third Street at five A.M."

"I'll have your brother pick you up and bring you to my apartment,"

Fernando said.

"Fine," Charlie answered back.

Handing me the radio, Fernando had a look of satisfied victory on his face. I took the walkie-talkie from his hand, and all of a sudden, he made me just want to...

"Well?"

"Well, what," I said.

"Come on, Joe," Fernando said. "Everything's laid out from A to Z. I need you there with us, Man."

I thought about Denise and the 'lil' guys. I thought about what a couple hundred thousand dollars could do to help us. I also thought about the consequences if something went wrong. But when I thought about my brother and the fact that he was going to be there, I was decided.

"Shit, Fernando," I said. "You're an asshole. Somebody's gotta be there to look out for Charlie. And you know I can't let Charlie be out there on his own. Count me in."

CHAPTER 21

That Sunday afternoon, Jose Soto declared war upon me. Strapped with high powered paint-ball guns and loaded down with bags of paint-ball ammunition, we stormed the abandoned building across from my house. Inside the dark, dank edifice, the battle raged. We hunted each other down in the corridors of hell. We used support beams and trash barrels as our cover. The layout inside was perfect. There were stairs that went to a second floor and a large basement. Ninety percent of the building was wide open like a warehouse. There were a few offices and a bathroom. We made use of it all, literally turning the walls into a canvas of splattered paint.

After killing each other a few times, we exited the building, looking like a couple of amateur painters. Paint was all over us. But it was fun.

"Hey, I gotta go over to Fernando's apartment. He's got some gear I want to see." I said to Jose, while walking to my house.

"Oh yeah. That's right," Jose said "You did tell me he's working at a paint-ball store. What's up? Do you think he'd mind if I come with you? I'd like to get some shit, too."

"I don't see why not. But I gotta warn you though, he asked about you."

"Me! Why me," Jose said.

"He says he wants to get to know you."

"Whatever," Jose said.

"He's not some kind of pervert is he?"

"I don't think so," I said with a devious look on my face. "At least I hope not."

"Go ahead with that shit, Joe," Jose said, laughing.

By the time we cleaned up and changed our clothes, it was almost three o'clock in the afternoon. I decided to take Denise's car, since it was always cleaner than mine. We drove into Merchantville, New Jersey and arrived at Fernando's apartment ten minutes after we left my house. We parked in the rear parking lot of the apartment building and walked up to Fernando's door. I knocked and a few minutes later a short chubby white lady answered.

"Hello!" She greeted, with a pleasant personality. Unsure if I had the right apartment. I was kind of hesitant to reply.

"Uh, hi. Is Fernando here?"

"Oh, no," she said. "He just stepped out. You must be, Joe."

"Yeah, that's me. How'd you guess?"

"I know your sister. She had a picture of you at her house," She said.

"My sister," I said. "Which sister?"

"Marissa," She said.

"Oh, well. It's definitely a small world. At least one of us knows the other." She smiled lightly at my feeble attempt at a joke.

"My name's Brenda. Me and Fernando are together. Would you like to come in? He should be back soon."

As pleasant as Brenda was, I still didn't know her. Besides, it's an unwritten rule that you never sit alone with another man's woman. It's just not a smart move.

"No thanks. Well just go grab something to eat real quick. We should be back in about twenty minutes."

Okay," she said. "See you when you get back."

Brenda closed the door and Jose and I walked back to the parking lot. Fernando was pulling in as we approached the car. He parked, and then walked over to us.

"Hey Joe. What's up? I see you got your friend here today."

"Yeah, we came to see you, but you weren't there. We figured while we waited for you to get back, we'd go get something to eat."

"Well, I'm back," Fernando said with a smile. "Did you come for the paint-ball gear?"

"Yeah. We both want to see what you have."

"No problem, come on; let's go back into the apartment. We can get something to eat later."

"I see you found him. That was quick." Brenda smiled, once we were back inside the apartment.

"Yeah, he caught us in the parking lot right before we left."

"Have a seat fellas," Fernando insisted.

Jose and I sat on the couch in the living room, while Fernando walked down a hall to the other end of the apartment. He disappeared only for a second, and when he returned, he had a brand new paint-ball gun in his hands. Excited, I had to let him know my thoughts.

"Is that an Angel?"

"That it is, my boy," Fernando said, handing the gun to me. "Wow! This thing is nice. I've seen them in magazines, but it's much nicer in my hands. The Angel's the best model on the market right now." "Yeah, it's the best, but it also costs more than a thousand dollars." Jose said.

Jose's eyes sparkled with excitement too. I could tell he wanted a chance to handle the gun himself. I handed it over to him, so he could get his fix. While the two of us marveled like a couple of kids over the paintball gun, Fernando walked over to Brenda. He whispered something in her ear, and I could tell by the look on her face that she wasn't too happy about what she was hearing. A moment later, she walked out the front door and was gone. It seemed kind of suspicions the way things went down, so I gave Fernando a side ways glance, but he never commented on it. He just turned toward the hall and disappeared again into the bedroom. When he returned again, he was holding a face mask, two boxes of paint-balls and a V-loader.

"Here you go," Fernando said. "This is the gear you wanted, Joe." "Cool. This stuff will definitely do the trick," I expressed, grabbing the Angel gun out of my hands.

"The gun is not for sale. That's my baby." Fernando said. "That's okay; your personal baby is out of my league. That damn thing costs too much. Even at half price."

"Fernando, do you have any more of those paint-balls and another Vloader here?" Jose said.

"I got 'em here. Sure."

"Good. I wanna buy some," Jose answered back.

I had my gear, and Fernando again disappeared and returned from his room. Once he was back in front of us, he fulfilled Jose's request. Had we gone to a store for the gear, we would've ended up paying a small fortune for the stuff we'd just bought for half price from Fernando.

Thank God for small tidings.

"Hey, guys," Fernando said, "follow me into the room. I got something to show you."

Curious, Jose and I followed Fernando down the hall and into the same room he had been disappearing into since we had arrived. When we walked in there was a closet wide open, directly in front of us. On the top shelf were enough ammunition boxes to load a small arsenal of weapons. There were at least five-thousand rounds packed away in that closet. Underneath the left corner of the shelves, we could see where he had some rifles sitting under the stacked boxes of ammunition. They were placed against the closet wall in a standing position. Near the wall, hung a couple of holstered hand guns on the mirror, there strap was secured by two corners of the mirror.

Fernando and I were one in the same. Well, almost. I was in love with guns: true, but from what I had seen in Fernando's room, he was just plain obsessed with guns. Yes, there is a difference; I can assure you of that. Some might think there's a fine line between a passion for something and an obsession, but there is a huge difference. Fernando was proud, with his chest stuck out; he appeared to be excited like a child about his new toys.

"Hey, guys. Check this out." He reached his hand up behind the boxes of ammunition and pulled out a pistol. Not surprising to me at all, Fernando handed it to me. "This is a Ruger," but he didn't stop there. He continued grabbing different types of guns from the shelf, as if he had an endless collection of them. "This one's a SIG-saur. And here's a Smith and Wesson."

I tried to hand Jose the Ruger, but he refused to touch it. He wouldn't touch any of the guns. I tossed each one on the bed as Fernando handed them to me. I had to admit that the guns turned me on. I was almost jealous, but I knew I couldn't have any of my own. Plus, with the kids around the house, I was okay with not having any around. I wouldn't have been comfortable with all that fire power around the 'lil guys. It also seems like Jose felt some kind of way about the weapons as well, because he just quietly stared. I exchanged a glance with Jose. I could see he wanted to get out of there, and I couldn't agree more.

"Hey Fernando, thanks for the display and all, but, uh, we gotta go. We've been playin paint-ball most of the day and we're hungry as hell. It's time to get something to eat."

"Sounds good to me. I'm hungry, too. I'll go with you." Fernando said, putting his pistols away. Fernando picked up the last pistol that I'd laid on his bed, but instead of putting it back into the closet, he tucked it into his waistline, under his shirt. He looked at me with a smile. "Okay. Let's go."

When we walked through the living room, I grabbed my bag with all the paint-ball gear in it and followed Fernando out the door.

"We can take my girl's Maxima." Fernando said, as we arrived at his car. Fernando opened the trunk, so I could throw my bag of gear in it, and Jose tossed his in behind mine. I walked around to the passenger door, opened it, and sat in the front seat. Jose sat in the back behind me.

"A Mickie D's will do the trick." I said, when Fernando got into the driver's seat.

"Okay, but first I want to show you something."

I should've known something was fishy when Fernando offered to drive us in his girl's car. Now he had us trapped with no place to go while he talked his non-sense. Even though Charlie and I had already agreed to go with Fernando's plan, I still felt a little animosity towards him for pushing the subject to the point that led us here in the first place. Not to mention, I never told Jose anything about what Fernando, Charlie and myself had decided.

"Fernando, damn man. We're just trying to go get something to eat."

"Just chill out, Joe. We'll get the food. It'll be quick, trust me. I just want to show you the spot."

"I've already seen the spot." I said, frustrated.

"Yeah, but that was before you decided to ride with me."

Jose tapped my shoulder from the back seat, when I turned to acknowledge him, he gave me a questioning look as if to say, what the hell is going on. I could only shrug and mouth the words, I'm sorry, although I knew that wouldn't be good enough, I knew that Jose understood the situation. Charlie and I had agreed to do the robbery with Fernando. And now here he was, caught up in the middle of it. Fernando drove steadily to the rest stop. He hadn't said anything more during the short ride, but when we arrived, he started right in with his plan.

"Okay, this is going to be real easy."

"So you've already told us." I said. Leaning back in his seat to be sure he could catch Jose's attention Fernando continued.

"Are you hearing this?" Jose just nodded his head silently. This wasn't what he had expected from this visit. Fernando continued. "Good we'll leave from my apartment early in the morning. We can avoid the toll booths by coming in from the rear side of the building. When we get around to the front, there'll be a camera on the corner. The truck will park on the other end of the parking lot away from the camera. We'll be in the full gear, masks, gloves, and everything. That way the camera really won't be a able to capture our images.

"If we're masked up and all, that's fine, but what if the camera gets the car on tape. That'll be a problem."

"I've already thought of that. We'll drive up in two different vehicles. We'll park one of the vehicles about a half a mile away in the residential area. When we hit the truck, we'll leave in one car, ditch it not too far from the other, and make a clean switch. Then I'll drive us home in the getaway car."

I listened, nodding my head as Fernando finished explaining his plan. It all sounded good, but I really wasn't feeling it in my heart. But there I was, listening, conspiring. Fernando asked Jose if he was going to join in. Jose never spoke, he just nodded in agreement. I could tell he was worried. Even when we finally made it to the fast food restaurant, the big man just sat quietly eating his food. I could see the consternation on his face. He wasn't comfortable, and I put him in this situation by bringing him with me to Fernando's.

When we arrived back at the parking lot of Fernando's apartment building, I got out of the car and walked to the rear to wait for Fernando to open the trunk. When he opened it, I grabbed our paint-ball gear and walked over to where I left Denise's car parked. Jose followed close behind. Just before I opened the driver's side door, Fernando called out to me.

"If anything changes, Joe. I'll call ya right away."

"Alright, Fernando."

"I'm sorry about that, but as you can see, Charlie and I decided to go through with Fernando's plan." I told Jose, driving back to my house.

"I see that, yes. But what made you change your mind?"

"Charlie's hurtin'. He really needs some help, and a hit like this could definitely aid him in his troubles. So, under Fernando's persistence, he finally broke down and said yes. I wasn't really trying to get down, but once Charlie made his decision, I knew I couldn't let him go alone. Besides, as much as I hate to say it, I could use the extra cash myself."

"I could use it, too," Jose said. "But damn, Joe. You've got Denise and the kids to think about. I have my girl, my son, and twins on the way. It's a big chance to take. Don't get me wrong, I need the money, too, but I ain't a hundred percent on this."

"But you're gonna go," I asked.

"I'm down with you, Joe," Jose said. "But I'm not tryin to get full of holes or end up locked down for a crazy number of years."

"Shit. You think I am," I said. "I'm just as nervous and as skeptical as you. But if Charlie is gonna be there, I gotta be there." I insisted. After making my last comment, we rode the rest of the way in silence. There was a lot for the two of us to think about, and there really wasn't much reason to keep talking about it. We were either going to do it, or we weren't. But as it was at that moment, we were going to rob an armored truck. When I pulled up in front of Jose's house, he never said a word. He simply opened the car door and left. Feeling the pressures of my decision, I rode the rest of the way home seriously thinking about the decision I had made. In four days we would all be faced with an armored truck, and a load of cash. I was not very confident. Something just didn't feel right.

That night, sleep eluded me. My mind was reeling, flashing visual images of the various scenarios that could take place on the day of the robbery. I lay in bed quietly, staring at Denise and her beautiful, sleeping face. Just the sight of her warmed my heart.

I quietly crept out of bed, careful not to wake Denise. I walked down the hall to check on the 'lil guys. The oldest, Melissa, was ten years-old. She lay silently in her bed, just barely a sound from her breathing. I then went to check on little Martin, who was only eight years-old. While I stood there at the door staring at him as he slept, I realized that the children really did count on me to be there for them. Yet, most importantly, Denise relied on me to be the man she deserved. Suddenly, I was fully aware of the fact, if something happened to me, the three of them would really be affected. It was easy money, and it could really help our little family, but was it really worth the risk?

"I can't do this," I whispered to myself, quickly returning to the bedroom and lay back down. I figured it would be best to radio Charlie as soon as possible to let him know that I was out. I didn't intend to tell Fernando anything. That asshole would be beating down my door until I changed my mind again. I knew I'd have to deal with him, but as long as he thought that I was in, I would at least get a few days of peace.

The next day, at five-forty P.M., Fernando called to reassure me that all was still good. I never said anything about me changing my mind. I didn't want to deal with any of his ranting. I knew he'd be upset and I knew it would be even worse for Fernando since Jose had told me earlier that day that he had also changed his mind. The only thing left for me to do was contact Charlie.

In the evening, around eight P.M., I did just that. I pulled out the radio from where I'd stashed it and radioed my brother.

"Hey, bro. You out there?" I said.

"Yeah. I'm here. What's up?" A few moments later, Charlie's voice answered back.

"I'm calling you about this thing we were supposed to go see. To be honest with you, it just doesn't feel right. I mean, the money sounds good and all, but I'm just worried about it."

"I've been thinking about it myself. I don't want to add to the pile of shit that I'm already in. I think we should forget about it, too. We should act like none of this ever happened. Besides, that gambling dept thing ain't our problem anyway.

We have enough of our own shit to worry about. I'm with you, I'm fallin' out"

Tuesday night, at six-fifty P.M., it was just two days before we were scheduled to move out on the armored truck hit, I decided to call Fernando. My intentions were to inform him that we had all changed our minds. I wanted to tell him that it would be best for the three of us not to be anywhere near that robbery, and that he might want to find someone else. Unfortunately, things didn't work out quite the way I had hoped.

"Hey, it's me, Joe." I said, when Fernando answered his phone. "Ooh, Joe. Good. I'm glad you called. Everything's set."

"Yeah, but...," Fernando quickly cut me off. "No worries," Fernando said. "Just show up at my place early." "Okay, but that's what I wanted to talk to...," I was interrupted.

"Gotta go, Joe. I'm busy right now, but I'll talk to you later." Then I heard a dial tone. He was gone. Damn! I thought to myself. The son of a bitch never gave me a chance to talk. I was left with everything that I wanted to say stuck in my throat. I hung up and just let it go. Fernando would know soon enough anyway, when nobody showed up for the robbery on the morning he expected us.

Wednesday, August 26, was the eve of what was supposed to be the first day of a new life, I found it quite surprising, or better yet, I felt relieved, that Fernando never bothered to call or stop by my house to confirm our plans. All the time and effort he put into convincing me to finally change my mind and go on this caper with him, and he couldn't even bother to find a reason to contact me. Not that it bothered me. I didn't want to see him anyway. That night I was in my bed, awake, thinking about what the next morning would hold for me. It was late, and I had to be up early, by seven

A.M., in order to be at work on time. I tossed and turned, stressing about what should've been, what could've been, and what was actually going to happen. I don't know what time I finally fell asleep, but what I do know is that when I woke up the very next morning, the morning of the robbery, I was late.

I was usually reliable when it came to work. Punctuality was always a plus in my life I felt. Yet, that morning, there wasn't much punctuality about me at all. After I woke up, I hurried to get ready. I put my clothes on, cleaned my face and brushed my teeth. I quickly ran down the stairs, flew out the front door, and damn near dove into my Camaro. Ten minutes later, I was speeding down the highway towards my work place. Much later than I had expected, my fears manifested themselves into reality. My cell phone rang.

"Where the fuck are you mother fuckers," Fernando screamed from the other end of the phone. "You were supposed to have been here hours ago. What the fuck is going on?"

I could tell he was quite upset, just as I assumed he'd be. My only response to him was cool.

"I'm late for work, Fernando." I hung up the phone.

Fernando had been a persistent pain in the ass for weeks, and now that he was pissed off, I really didn't want to have to deal with him. But Fernando will be Fernando, and without fail, he called again about fifteen minutes later. Though I didn't want to, I had to answer.

"You mother fucker."

"I don't want to talk to you right now. I'm trying to get to work." "I wanna fuckin see you."

"Not right now," I said, and hung up the phone.

I knew that the issue wasn't closed. I would have to deal with Fernando eventually, but at least for the moment, and most of the day, I didn't have to face him. It helped a lot that he didn't know where I worked. But, later that afternoon, around two o'clock, Fernando called my cell phone again. By that time I was on the job site. I knew he would be furious about me not showing up that morning, and even more pissed off because I was ignoring him. So, I kept my phone off and let my voice mail answer.

When I finally checked the message, it was of no surprise. He said that he wanted to see me right away. I already knew that, but I was trying to avoid him for as long as possible, so I didn't bother to call him back. Somehow, I had the feeling that I didn't have to; sooner or later he'd catch up with me. Unfortunately, he caught up with me much sooner than I had hoped. I'd made the mistake of turning my phone back on to make personal call, but I never turned it back off. At about four P.M., I answered my phone's ring without even thinking. It was Fernando.

"Where the hell are you?"

"I'm still at work, Fernando. Stop callin' me," I fussed, before hanging up the phone.

After our brief conversation, I couldn't help thinking to myself how upset this guy was. Did he want to find me to put a bullet in me? I had figured him for crazy, but would he be stupid enough to hunt me down and try to kill me? I didn't think so. Yet, how could I be sure? By the time I made it home from work that evening, it was close to seven. The loud roar of the V-8 engine from my Z-28 alerted the lil' guys to my arrival. As they have done so many nights before, they greeted me at the door with open arms and silly smiles on their faces. It was always a great feeling to be received by those who loved me, and it only confirmed my decision not to go through with the robbery.

It was good to be home, but I expected Fernando to come bursting through the door, bringing his chaos at any moment. It never happened. I washed up from work and changed my clothes. The whole time I was cleaning myself up; I anticipated Fernando's incessant honking of his horn or a persistent pounding at my door. By the time I was finished, Fernando still hadn't shown up. That evening with the family turned out to be a good one. Denise had worked a long day just as I had, but she still chose to cook for us instead of going out to eat. Without a doubt, she was a good woman. She worked full-time, and took care of me and the kids. Too bad there isn't over-time pay for women who work and tend to their families. Denise would have been stacked with money.

After the family meal, I helped Denise clean up the kitchen, and then we got the kids ready for bed. Once they were tended to and tucked in, I got myself ready for bed. I was tired from a long hard day's work. The landscaping for that day went well, but the lack of sleep from stressing all night the evening before had me dragging at work. I'm usually lively and on the ball, but that day had taken its toll on me. I had just laid myself down in my bed, thinking how great it was to be able to get through the evening without having to deal with Fernando and his crap. The moment my head hit the pillow, I heard an obnoxious honking in the streets right under my bedroom window.

"Shit," I whispered. Denise, who was laying in bed next to me turned over.

"What the hell is that?"

"It's Fernando," I said. "If I ignore him, maybe he'll go away."

"Not likely," Denise said with some frustration.

I stayed in bed, hoping he'd go away; but no such luck. The honking ceased for just seconds, only to be replaced by the pounding of our front door.

"Damn it," I said, getting out of bed to stick my head out of my window. I could see Fernando directly below me, standing at the top landing of the steps. He was directly in front of the door, so I hollered down. "Fernando, chill the hell out. Stop making so much damn noise. I'll be down in a minute."

"What the hell is wrong with that guy? Doesn't he know that people have to get up for work in the morning?" Denise said to me.

"The guy's fried in the brain," I said. "I'm gonna go take care of it. I'll be back in a few minutes."

I put on a pair of shorts and hurried downstairs to shut this guy up.

"What the hell's wrong with you? People are trying to sleep." I said, once I opened the front door. Fernando's face was twisted in anger.

"Get in the car." I didn't like the tone of Fernando's voice or the look in his eyes. He didn't say a word after that. He simply waved me on as he turned to walk back to his car. I wasn't so sure that I was doing the right thing by following him. I mean, I did slight him pretty bad, but I followed him to his car anyway. I knew I had to deal with him, so I figured it was best to just get it over with. However it turned out. I got into the passenger side and Fernando got behind the driver's side wheel, slamming the door shut. When he pulled away, he didn't say a word. I was waiting for him to say something, but we just drove in silence for about two hundred yards. Suddenly, we found ourselves in a spot that was a little more secluded than most in the neighborhood. Fernando parked the car, and then all hell broke loose.

Fernando slammed his hands on the steering wheel, which made me jump. His temper was evident. Screaming and cursing at me, he finally let me know just how he felt.

"You blew it! God damn it, you fuckin' blew it. Where the fuck were you guys? My guy was there. I was at the apartment waiting. That fuckin' truck was loaded with cash. You stupid fucks blew a great opportunity."

"Fernando, chill the hell out," I said. "Take it easy."

"Take it easy? Don't tell me to take it easy. Fuck you, Joe. My man was pissed."

I wasn't sure if this situation was going to get physical. Fernando may have been bigger than me, but that didn't mean that I was going to let him have his way with me.

"Man, you need to chill the fuck out, Fernando. You're taking your mouth a little too far."

"Why the fuck didn't you guys show up," Fernando said, his voice cracked as if he might cry.

"Hey Man, we just didn't want to do the shit, okay. No one was looking forward to the possibility of getting shot up or going to jail. You knew we really didn't want to do it anyway, we told you a hundred times. You just kept pressing the issue. This was something that you wanted, not us."

"You blew it for me, Joe. This was supposed to be my time to come out on top. God dammit! I have plans of my own, Joe. I want to go down to Florida and start over. I want to take Brenda and the kids and get the hell out of South Jersey. You fuckin owe me, Joe. When you needed money for your house, I looked out for you." There it was, the Devil's contract.

"Whoa," I said. "Don't go there with me. I would've never taken that money if I knew you were going to hold it over my head like this. Besides, twenty-five hundred dollars is nothing compared to the risks you're asking us to take. If I have to, I'll pay it off faster than we originally agreed, but I ain't gonna let you play that card with me on this."

"Get the walkie-talkie," Fernando said. "I want to talk to Charlie."

"Hell no! Ain't gonna happen. I'm not gonna bring Charlie up on the radio again for this shit."

"Then where the fuck does Jose live," Fernando said, with desperation straining his voice.

What the hell was up with this guy? What did it matter to him where Jose lived. He must really be crazy to think that after all the headaches he given me and my family, I'd actually send him to someone else's house just so he can subject them to the same torture, I thought before responding.

"What the hell do you care about where Jose lives? Forget Jose. I'm not telling you where he lives. You're not gonna go over there and drive him crazy like you've been doing to me. Shit, you don't even know the guy. And do me a favor; forget about me and Charlie going on this mission with you. You're gonna have to figure something else out." I sighed with a sorrowful expression. "Look. I'm tired. I don't want to hear about this shit anymore. I gotta get up early for work. I just want to get some sleep. Go home, Fernando."

Fernando had driven me almost two football field lengths away from my house. But I didn't care. I needed to be away from that fool, so without giving him a chance to respond to my statement, I got out of the car and started walking back to my place. The tires of Fernando's car screeched as he sped off. The smell of burnt rubber assaulted my nose, but at least he was gone. I wanted to get the hell out of the streets. I didn't need my neighbors thinking I had anything to do with that maniac. When I finally walked through my front door, all I cared about was getting to my bed. I walked up the steps and into my room. I crawled in between the sheets with Denise and hoped that Fernando and his madness was finally behind me this time.

CHAPTER 24

The next morning I felt good. It was a new day, and I was looking forward to it. When I left the house for work, I drove like any other day. On the ride to work, my cell phone interrupted my happy thoughts with its ringing. I looked at the caller ID. It was Fernando.

Shit! I thought to myself. Why is this asshole being so persistent? I didn't want to deal with him at all that day. I was feeling good and I wasn't going to let him ruin it for me. Unfortunately, his name alone brought about a mood change. Still, I was trying to maintain my contentment for the day, so I didn't bother answering the phone. I let the voice mail answer for me.

Actually I'd hoped that our discussion from the night before would've put everything back into its proper perspective. It seemed like Fernando lived in another world and in his mind the word "no" must have meant "I'll think about it." Maybe he was calling to make amends, I thought.

Highly doubtful.

Still, I must have been a gluten for punishment, because around ninethirty that morning, I broke down and returned his call. When Fernando answered his phone, I felt sympathetic.

"Hey, Fernando, It's me."

"I need to see you, face-to-face."

"Fernando, if it's about that other crap, I'm not giving you a second." "Come on, Joe," Fernando pleaded. "Just hear me out."

"Goodbye Fernando," I fussed before hanging up the phone. I

should've known better.

Later that night I was outside in front of my house, cleaning out my filthy Z-28. My car was the work car and the fellas, myself included, always left a mess on the floor after our lunch break. While I was ducked under the passenger's seat, picking up pieces of fallen fries and chicken nugget crumbs, I heard the roar of a large engine approaching from up the street. When I poked my head up from underneath the seat, I saw Fernando's white mustang pulling along side of the curb. He stepped out of the car and started walking over to me. I could see the protrusion of a gun that he regularly kept tucked in his waistline.

I stepped out of the car to meet him as he approached.

"Joe, I need to talk to Charlie. Please let me talk to him. I really need to get this thing over with, and soon."

"Fernando, what is your malfunction? I've already told you, no. What do I need to do to shake you loose?"

"Look. I understand your concern. You don't want to deal with armed guards or take any unnecessary risks. But Jesus, Joe. It doesn't get any better than this."

"What the hell are you talking about, now, Fernando," I said. "I've already heard all this shit before."

"No, you haven't," Fernando said. "You haven't heard it like this. Somehow my guy has things worked out to where he'll be making a run in the truck from point 'A' to point 'B'. He's not supposed to stop any where for anyone, for any reason. He's gonna be alone in the truck, but he's gonna make a stop at the rest area. He'll drive the truck up the turnpike so he can check for the state police Then he'll drive into the service plaza's parking lot. I have all the numbers to the police scanners, plus the ones I gave to you. We can listen for them throughout the entire area. Jesus Christ, Joe. It doesn't get any better than this."

"Fernando, you need to get the fuck out of here," I said. "No means no. How many times do I have to tell you? Just check your local rape hotline. They'll tell you. 'No means no'." Fernando let out a sigh of disappointment.

"Okay, Joe. But can you at least tell Charlie and Jose about the new set up?"

"Maybe," I said. "If I see Jose and if I get a chance to talk to my brother, I'll think about it."

I figured that I might as well tell him I'd think about it since he already thought the word 'no' meant "I'll think about it."

"Alright," Fernando said. "Good enough."

Fernando didn't bother to say goodbye. He just turned and walked back to his car. When he pulled away from the curb, he left the pavement unmolested. After Fernando was gone, I continued cleaning out my car. When I finally finished, I decided to take a drive. My need to take a ride was prompted by two reasons. One, I wanted to see if I could catch any cops tailing me that night, so I drove my car to Third Street. I kept my eyes busy looking around to see what I could see. When I parked the car along the curb on Third Street, I was facing Walnut Street. I hadn't noticed anything, so I turned off my lights and sat still for several minutes, watching the area through my rear-view mirrors and my windows. Nothing. Everything was still and quiet.

I reached under the passenger seat and pulled out the walkie-talkie; my second reason for wanting to take a ride. I had the walkie-talkie with me even while Fernando was present, but he didn't need to know that. After sitting still for a moment, I tried to make contact with my brother.

"Hey, it's me. Are you out there?" I waited, but received no reply, so I tried again, "Yo. It's me, man. Come back." Several moments passed in silence, and then I heard Charlie's voice.

"Yeah. I'm here. What's up?"

"Jesus, bro. This guy blew a gasket cause we didn't show up." "Yeah. So," Charlie said. "Did he get out of hand or something?" "I thought he was gonna take it there, but he didn't."

"So what's the problem," Charlie asked.

"After he cooled down for a couple of days, he showed up at the house again," I said. "He just left not too long ago. But he now says he has a different plan."

"How different," Charlie said.

"Are you really gonna consider this," I said.

"Just tell me what the hell he said," Charlie barked.

I explained the plan the way it was relayed to me. Charlie remained silent while he let every word sink in. Then when I was completely finished, he spoke.

"Alright. Let's look at this real good. We already think it's possible that the cops might be using him to bring me out into the open."

I said, "Yeah. That's a possibility. But I don't know. He's supposed to be in the car with us. It would be stupid for him to have us set up, because he'd be right there with us. If something goes wrong that puts him in the line of fire. Besides, he is family. That should mean something."

"I can't be sure myself. I could just be paranoid. But either way, I think we should leave it alone."

"I'm with you, bro," I said.

"Okay, then," Charlie said. "Is there anything else we need to talk about?"

"Nah," I said. "You just take it easy. Keep low and stay safe."

"Alright, I'll talk to you later," Charlie said.

And he was gone.

CHAPTER 25

I usually like to spend my weekends with Denise and the 'lil' guys. Sometimes we would do simple things like go to stores and window shop. Occasionally, we would break open our piggy banks and buy something. Usually, our budget would just allow us to dream. From time to time, we'd even end up on the scene of a yard sale. The yard sales were always more our pace. You can buy nice stuff at a yard sale for cheap. You know, "one man's trash..."

August 29 was a Saturday. My family and I were enjoying the day. We were cruising around hoping to find some late season sales. I had my phone off the night before and most of that morning, but when I finally turned it on, my voice mail indicator lit up.

Who would have guessed, it was my favorite cousin, and yes he'd left a message.

"Come on, Joe. I need you guys. Don't let me down."

How pathetic . I erased the message and enjoyed the rest of the day with my family. Later that evening, I drove by Jose Soto just a few houses from ours. He was on our block and was standing outside on the sidewalk, talking to a friend of his. When I pulled up in front of my house, I turned the car off and helped Denise gather our shopping bags. We trucked the 'lil' ones up to the house, but when I reached the top step of the front door, I stopped in my tracks.

"I'll be right back in a few minutes."

I handed Denise the bags in my hands. Giving me a quick kiss on the lips, she nodded okay. I walked up the block to where Jose was standing. When I attracted his attention, I waved him over to me. I did that because the people he was talking to had no business hearing what I was about to say. Meeting me on the side walk away from his friend, Jose extended his hand and I received it.

"What's up, Joe?" he said.

"Hey. I just returned from an outing with Denise and the kids." "Oh, yeah," Jose said "So what did ya do?"

"We just cruised around mostly," I said. "We were lookin' at shit we really can't afford."

"I know that feeling," Jose said.

"Yeah. How bout it," I said. "After awhile we just ended up kicking it at the park. We let the 'lil' guys run out some of that energy. Then we moseyed around some yard sales."

"Hmmmmm. Sounds like you had a good day."

"Hell, I'm domesticated now. What can I say? A family day is always good."

"Don't I know it," Jose said. "Other than that, what's been goin on?"

"Fernando's been goin on," I said. "What else?"

"Damn! That guy's still pressin'?"

"Man. He's driving me crazy. Ever since we didn't make it out to the last job, he's been hounding me."

"Fuck 'em. You weren't feeling it. I wasn't feeling it, and Charlie wasn't feeling it. It's over. Right?"

"Well, not quite," I said.

Jose looked at me as if he had just realized he was talking to a stranger. Truly, his expression was kind of comical, as comical as one could be under the circumstances.

"He came back the other night tellin' me about some new and improved plan he had," I said.

While I stood on the sidewalk speaking with Jose, I noticed a pair of head lights approaching our direction. It didn't take long for the roar of the engine to reveal who it was.

"Oh Shit!" And Fernando's car pulled alongside the curb, across the street from us. Following my gaze with his eyes, Jose smirked.

"What? What's wrong?" He asked.

"Here comes Mr. Never Quits, now."

"Oh," Jose frowned, watching Fernando cross the street.

Fernando had already vented on me, but that was the first time he had seen Jose since we stood him up. Showing his dissatisfaction, Fernando stepped in Jose's face and pounded a finger in his chest.

"You son of a bitch. Where the fuck were you? You left me hanging, too."

Jose didn't react to Fernando's threatening actions, he simply met Fernando's eyes with a hard stare. I could see Jose wasn't happy with the way Fernando acted towards him, but the big man kept his cool. It would not have been pretty if Jose had reacted. For whom I don't know, but be assured, it would've been a clash of two titans if they went at it with each other.

Instead, Jose just stood there quietly. Seeing he couldn't daunt the big man, Fernando quickly turned his attention to me.

"Let me talk to Charlie." He begged. I was frustrated with the fact that he couldn't leave well enough alone.

"Hold on." I walked down the street back to my place. When I reached the front door, I disappeared inside. When I re-emerged, I joined Fernando and Jose where I had left them. "Come on. Let's get into Denise's car. We can take a ride." Jose had a questioning look on his face. "You can come, too; if you want. I would prefer that you come with us," I said.

We all piled into the car, Fernando in the passenger's side and Jose in the back. I drove us close to the old Ben Franklin Bridge and found a place to park. I pulled the walkie-talkie out of my coat pocket and I hailed my brother over the radio waves.

"Yeah. What's up, now," Charlie's voice answered back.

"Ah, man," I said, "I've got the fellas here again. Big cuz is determined to talk to you again."

"Okay. Put him on." I handed Fernando the radio.

"Hey cousin. What's going on," Fernando said.

"What the hell do you want now?" Charlie's voice was dry, and he sounded irritated. Dealing with Charlie more delicately than he did with me and Jose, Fernando spoke up.

"You guys kind of left me hangin on this thing, Man."

"Yeah, well. It just didn't feel right to us," Charlie said. "There's not much else to it."

"Okay, I can accept that," Fernando said. "But I've got something a little different for you."

Fernando explained the new plans to Charlie, just as he had earlier explained them to me. He told Charlie the new particulars of the circumstances. He said how the driver would be alone and that a special trip would be made that no one was supposed to know about. The risks were minimal.

Charlie listened quietly as Fernando talked.

"I'm the one taking the biggest risk here," Fernando said. "Nobody knows who any of you are except me. And I'm family, so there's no way I'm gonna to turn you into the cops. Besides, my dad would kill me if I sent his nephews to prison. I'm gonna be right there on the front line with you guys. We're going to go at this thing together." Again, Charlie fed in.

"When do you plan on doing this?"

Excited about the possibility of Charlie changing his mind, yet again, Fernando became more animated in his explanation.

"My guy said he'd be at the rest stop on Tuesday, September first. He'll be there at nine A.M. All we have to do is show up and make it obvious that he's out gunned. No muss, no fuss. No shoot out, no one gets hurt.

"I'll drive us there from my apartment, and I'll drive us back to my apartment when it's done. Nothing bad is going to happen."

We all sat in silent anticipation as Charlie brooded over Fernando's proposition. After several minutes, Charlie had an answer for him.

"Okay, man. You got me. I'll be there."

"Really? No bullshit this time?" Fernando said.

"Really," Charlie said. "No bullshit."

"Hold on a second," Fernando said to Charlie. Looking at me, he said,

"Well? What's it gonna be? Charlie's in again. We can still get this thing done and get paid."

"Damn it," I said softly. I had battled with Fernando, as well as my own demons for weeks. I knew there was a reason that we kept saying no, and it was difficult to be considering this after so much headache. There I was again, Charlie had made the plunge, and I just couldn't see myself not being there to watch his back. With a feeling of defeat, I gave my reply.

"Alright Fernando; you win. I'll be there." I said as Fernando then turned his attention to Jose.

"What about you? It's a once in a life time chance. Are you gonna be there, or are you gonna leave your boys hangin'?"

Jose sat quietly, thinking of his options.

"I feel like I'm on a roller coaster. One minute we're up, the next we're down. It looks like for the moment, we're up again. I won't leave ya hangin, Joe. I'm in." Talking back into the radio, Fernando gave the update.

"Alright. Everybody's down for Tuesday. This is gonna happen and we're gonna come up big. I'm leaving this shithole state once I have my share."

"Yeah, whatever," Charlie said. "Just make sure you pick me up at Third Street by the bakery at four-thirty in the morning. I'll be waiting there on Tuesday."

Showing his uncertainty with Charlie's intentions, Fernando confirmed. "You're gonna be there, right?"

"I've already told you I'm in," Charlie said. "Just be there."

We heard a slight click sound come from the radio and Charlie was gone. My mind was whirling. I felt like I had just experienced déjà vu. We had the same conversation a week ago, but I knew this time was different. There wasn't going to be any backing out. We were going to rob an armored truck.

My stomach felt sick.

Monday, August 31, was one day before the caper, I felt like an AT&T operator. Fernando rang my phone so much I thought the thing would vibrate itself to pieces. He definitely wanted to be sure that we didn't leave him out to dry again.

During our last conversation that evening, I told Fernando, "It's a go. Stop buggin' out. We'll be at your apartment tomorrow morning."

September 1, 1998, the big day. I didn't sleep well the night before. The butterflies weren't only fluttering in my stomach, but they created a tsunami of stress. What little bit of sleep I did get, only made me that much more groggy. I peeled myself out from between the sheets that morning nonetheless. It was three-thirty in the morning, and I had to pick up Jose at his house. I knew timing was important and by four A.M., I was out the door, heading to Jose's place.

I wasn't one hundred percent sure that he would actually be there waiting, or even come outside to join me. I knew the truth would be told when I arrived at his house. Of course, it was. When I pulled up in front of Jose's front door, everything was quiet and still. After waiting several minutes, Jose appeared at his door.

He walked out and got into the car. When he sat in the front seat, he looked flushed.

"What happened to the interior light? Is it broken?"

"No, I just took it out to keep the lights off when we open the doors." "Hmm, that'll work," Jose said. "Okay then, are we ready?" "I still have to go pick up Charlie."

Meeting up with Jose was easy. No one was out to get him. Picking up Charlie on the other hand was a bit scarier. A slew of paranoid thoughts danced around in my head. What if a jump out team of police were there waiting to pounce on Charlie the minute he showed himself? It was a chance that we were all about to take.

When I arrived at Third Street, I slowly pulled up passed the bakery, parking beneath a small tree that stood close to the edge of the side walk. I flicked my head lights on and off twice, then I shut them off completely. Immediately, Jose and I saw a silhouetted figure at the end of the side walk walking towards the car. We sat quietly waiting to confirm what we already thought was Charlie. When the figure walked within ten feet of the car, I could easily see that it was my brother. He strolled as if everything was normal. He had no worries. He walked straight to the back of Denise's four door sedan. When he got into the car, he laid across the back seat, hiding himself from anyone's sight. He lightly placed his hand on my shoulder.

"Let's go, guys." After I pulled away from the curb, I was anxious to talk to him.

"Man! It's good to finally see you again, bro." Not once did I turn my head back or even take my eyes off the road.

"You, too," Charlie said. "Just drive straight. We still have a long day ahead of us."

It was an eventless ride to Fernando's apartment. I was without a doubt a nervous wreck. I was sure to follow all the traffic laws. I wasn't giving anyone an excuse to even take notice of me.

"I know we're all thinking it, but I'm gonna say it. If this thing is a setup, I don't want any of you two to do anything stupid. The police want me, so if they're there, no point in either of you getting yourselves fucked up over it." Charlie said, before we arrived at Fernando's place.

"I could pull off and speed away if we see it coming in time," I said.

"No. If it happens, it happens. Besides, ain't Fernando gonna be driving?"

"Oh, yeah. That is the plan, isn't it?"

"Well," Charlie said, "if they decide to jump out on us at Fernando's apartment, you and Jose ain't really gonna be in too much trouble. But if they're waiting for us at the rest stop, you'll both be charged with weapons possession. We don't have anything special as far as guns go, so it shouldn't be too bad for the two of you."

"Either way, we're taking a pretty big risk with this thing," I said. "Are you sure it's worth it?"

"I need a good lawyer. And if we are just being paranoid and this thing does go off good, we'll be sitting pretty, and I'll be able to fight that damn bogus shooting charge on that cop."

Once we arrived at Fernando's apartment, I slowly pulled the car into the parking lot. Jose and I both surveyed the area carefully, but we didn't see any signs of cops. I parked the car and shut off the ignition.

"Fernando gave me his key to the front door. We can just walk in. Charlie, he knows how you feel about being seen, so there won't be anyone inside except for him. You guys ready?"

"As ready as we're ever gonna be," Charlie said.

Just before I cracked my door open, movement on my left caught my attention.

"Hold on. Don't open any doors," I said.

I looked hard and something caught my eye. It was Fernando's girlfriend Brenda, and her two children. They were walking towards a car. Fernando was behind, pushing them along. I could see from where I sat that Brenda was flustered. Of course, that issue was between the two of them, whatever it was. There was a wanted fugitive in the back of my car; so, I wasn't interested in drawing any attention to myself. Brenda packed her children into the car and drove away. Fernando stood at the empty parking space for a moment, watching as the tail lights of Brenda's car faded. As he walked over towards where we were parked, my eyes followed him. I hadn't even realized that he saw us, but apparently he had.

Fernando slowly walked to the back of the car, and once he arrived, he knocked against the trunk. He waved us out of the car. We all exited, and the four of us walked into apartment three without incident.

"Have a seat, fellas. Just relax for a few minutes, we still have some time." Fernando said, walking inside the apartment. Jose and I sat down on the couch. Charlie remained standing.

"Talk to me cousin. How the fuck you been?" Fernando said, talking to Charlie.

"I've been okay."

"You've been quite the talk. There are a lot of people who are worried about you."

"I can't help that; but, I bet there are plenty of people who would like to see me underground. The way I take it, they've made me public enemy number one."

"This is true," Fernando said. "We're gonna fix that, right?" "We're gonna do something," Charlie said.

"So, where have ya been all this time?"

"I've been around," Charlie said, guarded about his answer. "Fair enough," Fernando agreed. "Well, wherever you've been, you sure look like you've been eating good." Then Fernando then turned to me, "Joe, ya wanna go get our second car?"

"Uh, okay. Where is it?"

"It's in the neighborhood, not far from here."

"You'll have to be a little more specific than that, Fernando." "Do you remember that nut, Alex," Fernando asked.

"Yeah. That crazy bastard who's always into something?" "That's the one," Fernando said. "Do you remember where he lives down there on Pine Street?"

"I know where he lives. But I never really made it a point to visit him." "You don't have to visit him. The car is parked a few houses away from his place."

"Damn, Man. We just came from down there. So give me the keys, and I'll go back and get it"

"Well, that's gonna be somewhat of a problem."

"Why," I asked.

"There ain't any keys," Fernando said. "What do you mean, 'there ain't any keys,' I said. "I thought you said you had somebody at City Select that could help you out."

"That deal sort of fell through. I had to resort to plan B." "So what's plan 'B'?"

"Well, it's not complicated. Just pull up the rod on the left side of the steering wheel and it'll start."

"Oh, that's nice. Is it on the hot sheet yet?"

"At this point, I honestly don't know if it is or isn't," Fernando said. "That's not good enough," I sarcastically said.

"Just drive the speed limit. Don't do anything stupid and you should be fine," Fernando replied.

"What kind of car am I looking for?" I asked.

"It's an old tan, four door Buick with a V-8 engine. It has Philly plates.

You'll know it when you see it."

"Okay." I stood up from the couch. I looked to Jose, who was paying close attention. "I'm gonna need you. Come on." Jose stood up nodding his head in acknowledgment.

"How do you want to do this?"

"You'll drive Denise's car. I'll ride in the passenger seat. When we find the Buick, I'll get out and drive it back here."

"You guys be careful. And keep your eyes open," Charlie said. "You bet," I replied, following Jose out the apartment door.

Within minutes, we made it to Pine Street. When we got there, everything was still quiet. That early in the morning, the city was always dead. The sun hadn't even started to rise yet, which left the creatures of the streets slumbering.

If there were tumble weeds in South Jersey, we would have seen them rolling through the streets that day. Alex's house was on the right side of the street, so I motioned so Jose would see it.

"There's the house," I pointed up ahead of us.

"Okay, we found the house, but Fernando didn't say what side of the street the car was parked on."

"I guess he didn't, did he? Shit. I forgot to ask. Well, it can't be too hard to find. He said it is a four door sedan. Tan in color with Philly plates. Just cruise down the block a little. We'll know it when we see it."

Jose drove Denise's car at a crawl through the street. We both watched our own sides of the road, looking for the car. About a block down from Alex's house, we found the Buick parked on the right side of the street.

"There it is," I said.

"I see it."

Drive down one more block," I said. "I want to see if the car is being watched."

Driving passed the Buick, Jose focuses in on it.

"Man, cops could be anywhere in any of these buildings, looking out the window. We'll never see them."

"I still need to check to see if I catch someone slipping," I insisted, as we rode down to the end of the block. I couldn't see anything out of the ordinary, but Jose was right. Cops could've been hiding behind anyone of those windows. "Alright, turn around and let's do this. If there is anybody watching, I guess we'll find out soon enough."

We turned the car around and drove back to the Buick. When Jose neared the vehicle, it was on his side of the road, so he was able to pull into the empty space directly behind it. I put on my black leather driving gloves and stepped out of Denise's car. I walked up to the driver's side door and gently pulled the handle. It opened without a problem. When I sat behind the steering wheel, I could see where someone had really torn the steering column to hell. As I shut the car door, my hands fumbled around the devastated column, searching for the rod Fernando told me about. I finally found it after several agonizing minutes. I grabbed hold of the rod and pulled it towards me. The Buick's engine fired to life.

I let the engine warm itself up, while I checked the lights. First, I tested the brake lights, can't go around in a stolen car without brake lights. I couldn't see them for myself from the driver's seat; so I had to get Jose to look at everything from his view for me. I could see Jose through my rear view mirror sitting in the car behind me. He was giving me the okay sign. Together, we checked all the turn signals and drive lights.

When all systems were checked, Jose pulled Denise's car up alongside the Buick. He nodded to me, motioning for me to take a small lead. Satisfied all was okay, I slowed down, and then followed behind him a couple of car lengths. We'd already prearranged a warning system. If he flashed his brake lights quickly twice, then I would know that there was a cop nearby. If a cop noticed the car, the plan was, I would ditch the car, then get out and just walk away. Fortunately, it never came to that. We made it back to Fernando's apartment without any problems. When we walked through the front door, a sense of relief washed over me. I was happy to be back indoors. For some reason, I felt too exposed out there in the street. Inside the apartment, I reclaimed my spot on the couch. When I looked around the living room, I noticed Charlie wasn't anywhere in sight. I felt a brief sense of paranoia, but then I heard a noise come from down the hallway. Walking out of the bathroom and up towards us was a smiling Charlie.

"I'll take it everything went good."

"Yeah. Everything's cool. It rides smooth, all the lights and stuff work on the car, and there's plenty of room inside for the four of us. Man, as long as no one recognizes it as a stolen vehicle, we should make it to the rest stop just fine."

"Good," Charlie said. "That's what I like to hear."

"Hey guys. Come here for a minute." Fernando yelled, sitting at his dining room table. We each took our positions, standing around the table. Fernando had a blank sheet of paper resting flat on the table. He also held a pen in his hand, which he used for sketching. "Alright, this is the main building. Over there, diagonally across from the corner are gas pumps. We are gonna come up from behind the main building here," he pointed. " We're gonna use this rear service road," he lifted his hand to his face to think.

"Yeah. That's the one we used when you showed us the place, ain't it?" Jose said.

"Yeah, that's the one," Fernando confirmed. "When we drive up the service road, we'll come to the entrance of the rear parking lot. To our left, there'll be some trees and a grassy area with some picnic tables. On the other side of the grass plot, will be some phone booths. They'll be right there at the end of the building.

Once we drive into the parking lot, we'll park the car in the immediate corner. We'll back in so that we can keep the building and the phone booths in sight. Once we're parked, I'll get out of the car and walk over to the phones. From there, I'll be able to see the front parking area and you. I'll have to jump a small fence, but that'll be nothing. On the other end of the building from where I'll be standing, there's a camera. My friend will end up in the center of the building. He'll come through and park in the front."

"Wouldn't there be a camera at the other end of the building, too?" Jose asked.

"My information says that there's only one camera on the front corner of the building. It's facing the pumps. I was never told about another camera. So that's what I'm going by." Jose nods in acknowledgment, and Fernando continues. "Now, I also have a Chevy Lumina van that we'll use for our getaway car. We'll drive both vehicles up to the general area of the service plaza. There are some houses around there about a quarter mile away from the rest stop. We'll park the van there, and I'll get into the Buick with you guys." Fernando pauses to briefly think, and then he continues. "Okay, yeah... We'll leave the van there and drive to the rest stop. Hopefully people won't connect it to the robbery. As soon as we pull into the rear parking area, we'll park in the first parking space to our right and I'll get out to walk over to the phone booths. Like I already said earlier, you'll be able to see me, and I'll be your eyes to the front parking lot from where I'll be standing at the booths. When my boy pulls up, I'll take my hat off, letting you guys know it's time to move. You'll pull the car around to the front of the building and drive up on the armored truck. From that point, we'll let him know who's in charge and take our riches. I mean, it's not like he'll bother to resist anyway."

"Sounds good, but what about all the people that'll be around? Is it gonna be packed or what?"

"According to my guy, it's really not that busy that time in the morning. Besides, when we have the money, we'll quickly switch everything over into the getaway van. That should buy us enough time to duck out and make it back to the apartment. As long as the van stays out of sight, we should be fine."

"Sounds like one hell of a mission," Charlie said. In a somber tone.

"It is a mission, a million dollar mission." Fernando, stated, looking at each of us as we stood around the table listening. "Is everybody straight on how we're gonna do this? Do ya understand the plan, or do we have to go over it again?"

The three of us nodded our heads in understanding. When Fernando was satisfied that the four of us were all on the same page, he smiled.

"Good," he said, rising from his seat at the table.

Our eyes followed him as he walked across the living room to a closet by the sofa. He reached his hand into the closet and pulled a black duffle bag out, and then another. They looked heavy and when they thudded on the floor, my interest was elevated.

"What the fuck is that," I said. Fernando looked toward me with a mischievous grin on his face. When he opened the bags, my jaws damn near hit the floor. "God damn, Fernando. What the hell are you trying to do, go to war," I queried.

"Nah, I just wanna establish that we can have control over the situation."

"Well, shit. Your guy's in on it. So we don't need all that. There's a small arsenal in that bag."

"Yo. Man, we aren't taking all that shit." Jose said.

"Yes we are. We need to make it look real, so that my guy doesn't come under any pressure. He can't be linked to this at all."

"Well, we don't really want to be linked to it either," I said. Fernando shrugged his shoulders.

"Then let's do this thing right." He then opened the bag. I could see the hardware packed inside from the opened top. This bag was loaded. There was a tactical swat vest, the pockets were loaded with ammunition. I could see a bullet proof vest and a J-15 assault rifle. There were multiple hand guns of different makes and models. Hell, he even had a Mac-11 with a silencer.

"Jesus, Fernando," My eyes widen "This is overkill."

"Look, we're about to go rob an armored car. We can't show up like we're half assin' it." Fernando fussed, turning back to the closet to pull out even more stuff. "Here," he said, and tossed each one of us a walkie-talkie radio, a police scanner and a mask for our faces.

He wasn't kidding when he said that he had everything we needed for the job. This guy was on something extra. While I was contemplating Fernando's zealous gun obsession, my stomach reminded me that I hadn't eaten anything that entire morning. My nerves were wrecked, this is true, but nothing can ever go well on an empty stomach.

"Do you have any orange juice or anything in the 'fridge'?" I asked.

"Hell yeah, bro, I'm hungry," Charlie said.

"I'm hungry, too. You got anything to eat in there?"

"Me too, Fernando," Jose said. "I'm hungrier then hell."

"Don't really have anything in the 'fridge' for you guys," Fernando said. "Most of that stuff is for the kids, but we have time. I can run to the store and grab something for us." Fernando reached into his pocket and pulled out a large roll of money. "All I have are hundreds and fifties. Anybody have something smaller?" I reached into my pocket and pulled out my wallet.

"Here, I got a twenty. That should cover us." Fernando took the twenty.

"I'll get us some breakfast sandwiches. I'll be back soon." And he walked out the door. When Fernando left, Jose decided to express himself.

"Yo! I don't know about this. Man, look at all that shit he's got. What the hell do we need all that for?"

"We'll take some of it, but leave the rest. No one can move around with all that shit anyway." Charlie said. I turned from the window to talk with Charlie, but I saw that he wasn't there in the living room any longer. I knew Jose was in the bathroom, but where did my brother go? I walked down the hallway into Fernando's room and saw him standing in front of the window, looking out onto the main street behind the apartment building.

"What's up, bro?" I said. Charlie, still staring out the window, barely gave me eye contact.

"This would be a good time for them to hit us, don't you think? We're the only three here. Fernando left. Brenda and the kids are gone. And we are actually here like sitting ducks. There's only one way in or out of here."

I didn't really know what to say.

"Damn!" I muttered.

"I'm just watching the street for the boys in blue. Bro, I'm hoping like hell that they ain't comin' to kick down the doors and lay us all down on the floor." Charlie said.

CHAPTER 28

Sitting in the living room, the three of us waited for Fernando to return with our food. We had arrived at the apartment at five that morning. It was now six-thirty-five A.M., and S.W.A.T. still had not raided the place. We figured that was a good sign. If anything would've happened, it should've already gone down. We heard the sound of a vehicle pulling into the parking area behind Fernando's place. Still jumpy, Charlie quickly went to the window to look out.

"It's Fernando. He's back with our food," he said.

"It's about time, I feel like I'm about to eat myself from the inside out." "So far, everything seems to be on the up and up. No jump out boys.

But if at any point the police do happen to show up, I meant what I said earlier. Don't do anything stupid. You minimize your damages as much as possible. The worst case scenario, Joe and Jose, you get charged with harboring a fugitive and possession of a gun. I don't plan on taking all that shit Fernando has there."

Jose and I looked at each other and shook our heads right as Fernando entered the house. Immediately he entered the living room and noticed the bag had not been touched.

"What's up you guys? I thought you'd have all the toys out by now, tinkering with everything."

"It's still pretty early. What time are we actually gonna leave from here?" Charlie asked.

"Around eight-thirty or so; it's only about a fifteen minute ride to the rest stop, so we can take our time. No need for speed or anything. Besides, we don't want to get there too early. If we're just hanging around waiting for too long, we'll draw too much attention to ourselves."

"Man, fuck all that for now," Jose said. "What'd ya get us to eat?"

From a bag in his hand, Fernando pulled out sweet buns and coffee cakes and handed us our food. Whatever happened to the breakfast sandwiches, I don't know, but something was a whole lot better than nothing. Fernando then passed out some juices. I couldn't help but notice that Fernando never handed me my change from the twenty I gave him.

"Come on guys," Fernando said, walking over to the bag on the floor. "Let's check all this shit out." He grabbed the bag and dumped the contents out on the floor. Charlie and I immediately put our gloves on. Jose found a pair that was dumped on the floor from the bag and he put those on. All of our fingerprints were on record. There was no need for us to be careless with those weapons. You never can be too sure of exactly where a gun has come from.

Jose took a seat on the sofa and Charlie and I positioned ourselves on either side of Fernando. Kneeling down in front of the bag, Fernando randomly chose what he wanted for each of us. To Charlie, he gave a Ruger GP-100 .357

magnum with a holster equipped with a pouch. Inside the pouch, there were two speed loaders for the revolving cylinder of the magnum.

Jose was given a holster with a Berretta 92-F 9mm Semi-automatic. Fernando also gave him a belt with two pouches. I also received a holster, before he tossed me two pouches with ammunition in them for the Ruger P89-DC 9m.m that fit just right into the holster.

"What about vests," I said. Before I could fully complete my thought, Fernando threw me a black tactical vest equipped with a lot of pockets. "Okay. That'll work."

"Hold on." Fernando stood up over the bags. He walked down the hallway and disappeared into his bedroom. When he returned, he was holding two bullet proof vests in his hands. To me, Fernando threw a dark blue Point Blank vest. I was somewhat stuck with a stupid look on my face. I mean, what was I suppose to do with a tactical vest and a bullet proof vest? That makes for a tight fit, and a lot of extra added weight. Fernando tossed Charlie the other bullet proof vest. It was solid gray in color. For Jose, Fernando picked up a green bullet proof vest that had been laying on the floor with the rest of the stuff, and threw it to him. Walking up to me, Fernando took the black vest that he had initially given me. He had about twenty magazines that weren't loaded.

"Hold up! I gotta go back to get the rest of the ammo. Grab all the empty clips and get them together. I'll be right back." Fernando expressed. Charlie, Jose and I looked at each other with a confused expression as if to all say at one time, what now and what the hell was wrong with him, we all seemed to be thinking. More ammunition, was he kidding? Apparently not.

The three of us gathered up the empty magazines while we waited for Fernando to come back into the living room.

When all the clips were ready, Jose decided to try on his green vest. He was a big guy. I watched as he suffered in his own personal battle, trying to put on the small vest. I could see that Jose wouldn't be happy with the thing, if he ever got it on, and thankfully he never did. He gave up his struggle, accepting the fact that his battle was lost. The vest was just too small. Frustrated, he threw it onto the floor.

"That damn thing ain't gonna fit me."

Fernando returned from his bedroom. In his hands, he carried ammunition boxes for a 308 AK assault rifle. What a fanatic. Not hiding his frustration, Jose confronted Fernando.

"No way this vest gonna fit me. Man, it's too damn small." "Try this one, Jose." I lifted my blue vest into the air.

Fernando, who was closest to me, grabbed the vest out of my hand and passed it over to Jose. Jose wrapped the vest around his broad shoulders. The vest fit. Finally, he'd found himself a match. Fernando picked up Jose's discarded vest and tossed it to me.

"Here. Try it on." I put the vest on. It was a little heavy, uncomfortable even, but it fit.

"There's a lot of shit here. How the hell are we gonna carry all of it?" I asked.

"We're gonna pack it back into the bags," he insisted, throwing me a couple of AK magazines. "Here help fill these things up. Come on guys, let's get this done."

For some time, we all fumbled around with loose rounds, stuffing them into the clips. I couldn't figure out why we had all that fire power. It just seemed like such over kill, but like an automaton, I just went along with my cousin. After most of the magazines were finally loaded and ready, we began to fiddle around with our equipment. Jose was trying on his belt. Of course, it wouldn't fit at first. Fortunately, he was able to extend it another twelve inches in order to get it around his thick waist. Since I'm left handed, I had to readjust my belt, so the gun and holster would be positioned on my left side. Charlie had to adjust his own belt to fit his right hand. When my gear was all set, I let the gang know.

"I'm ready to go."

"Why don't you put the black vest on?" Fernando asked.

"God damn, Fernando, I can barely move with all the shit I have on now. If I load myself up anymore, how the hell am I supposed to get to the car, let alone pull off this crazy robbery?" Fernando threw me a red wind breaker.

"Here, use this to cover the gear, it shouldn't weigh much." Fernando said to me. "When we get to the rest stop, we don't want any of our equipment to be hidden. We'll all take off our jackets that'll be hiding our gear. That way, anyone at the armored truck who sees us full blown, won't have any doubts in their minds about how real this shit is. But we gotta take everything we've got here, Joe. So please, put the vest on, too."

Reluctantly, I did as Fernando asked. I put the black vest over the green bullet proof jacket. I then slipped on the red wind breaker. I stood up from the couch and walked around the living room, trying to loosen up all that gear. It was without a doubt heavy, and restricted my movement. But we were just trying to make it all look good, right? We needed to be sure that Fernando's friend didn't look suspicious, right?

When Fernando turned to walk down the hall to his bedroom again, I chose to follow.

"Man, what the hell are you doing now, Fernando," I said, walking behind him.

Once inside the room, Fernando started grabbing more 9mm rounds and more loaded clips. I noticed a knife sitting on his bed. Attracted to it's workmanship, I picked it up. After admiring the blade, I tossed it back on the bed.

"Yo! We've got too much shit as it is." I said to him.

Fernando never bothered to acknowledge my comment; he simply turned and walked out of the bedroom. Again, I followed him back up the hallway towards Charlie and Jose. I could feel all the weight from my gear weighing heavily on my body. It was already tiring out my muscles. It felt like something the Marines would train with. With all that gear I had on, I knew if I had to make a fast break, I wasn't going to get far. Hell, exhaustion from the weight was sure to tire me out quickly. But once we made our move on the armored truck, I had every intention on staying as close to the car as possible. You know, just in case something went wrong.

The four of us gathered once again in the living room. Fernando tossed me a knife. It was the same one I had tossed back on his bed in his room. I never even saw him pick it up. I looked at Fernando questioningly, but he hadn't paid me any attention. I just shrugged my shoulders and strapped to my belt. I liked the way it felt.

"Fernando, this is crazy. There's no way we'll be able to carry all this stuff. It's too much. This shit's just gonna end up slowing us down." Charlie spoke up.

The total inventory in one bag, other than the military type clothing was; twenty magazines for an AK-47 assault rifle; twenty magazines for a J-15 Eagle Arms assault rifle, all packed in the bag with more pouches of ammunition. In the other bag were the J-15 and the AK-47 themselves. The Mac-11 automatic equipped with a silencer and clips of ammunition was neighbor to the two assault rifles. The hand guns that had arrived with the big guns were already strapped to our persons. It really did look like we were about to go to war. Pulling the clothes out of one of the bags, Fernando replied.

"We'll be alright," he started, tossing items to Jose and Charlie. "Here, put those on."

Jose slipped a black military shirt on over his head to cover his vest. He also put on a matching pair of black pants. Charlie was given a black hooded windbreaker and black windbreaker pants to match. They both looked like ninjas. I was the only one out of place with my blue jeans and red windbreaker on. Other than weighing too much, I was set to go. Fernando was geared up with his plain white bullet proof vest under his t-shirt. He placed a green and yellow baseball cap on his head and was armed with a forty caliber glock. As an afterthought, I checked the walkietalkie that Fernando had given to me. It was a good thing I did, too. It could've been an extremely bad situation to get out in the field and learn the damn thing didn't work at a critical moment.

"Fernando, what's the deal? The radio doesn't work."

"Don't worry about it," Fernando said.

"Don't worry about it," I said. "What the fuck do I have it for, if I don't have to worry about it?"

"Your radios just for show. I have a working radio, and Charlie has the other one."

"Just for show," I said, frustrated. "Then what the hell is the point in carrying all the extra weight?"

"It adds to the realism," Fernando said with a smirk.

"Adds to the realism my ass, it'll really be shitty if we need the damn things and only two out of three are working."

"Don't worry, everything's gonna be fine," Fernando said. "Okay, here's how we're goin to do this. Joe, you're gonna leave with me. We're going to walk into the parking lot, down to the vehicles. I'll jump into the van; you'll get into the Buick. When I feel everything is clear, I'll call Charlie on the walkie-talkie and tell him and Jose to come out," he gave orders to bringing our focus back on the mission. "Charlie, you're in the Buick with your brother. Jose, you will be in the van with me. Everybody all set?"

The three of us all nodded in agreement. The time was here. I could feel the tension in the air and my nerves were working overtime. My stomach felt tight as if it was being twisted into knots. By the end of the next forty-minutes, we were going to be robbing an armored truck. The uncertainty carved out a hollow hole in my chest.

"Hell, I'm as ready as I'm gonna get. Let's get this thing over with."

"Let's go," Fernando said, leading the way out of the door.

Before exiting the apartment, I noticed Fernando left his glock on top of the television. I found it quite peculiar that everyone was armed to the gills, but Fernando saw fit to leave his side arm behind. I never did confront him about it, although seeing it now in hindsight; I realize how foolish it was not to. Life was peculiar, right?

Outside in the parking lot, I walked down to the Buick and entered the driver's seat. I sat there as I watched Fernando walk about ten more spaces to get to the van. I pulled the rod along the inside of the steering column and the Buick fired right up. While I sat in the idling car to let the engine warm up, I looked over to where Fernando was sitting in the van. I could see that he had a pained expression on his face. Leaving the Buick engine running, I stepped out of the car and walked over to the van. When I knocked on the driver's side window, Fernando rolled it down.

"What's up?" Visibly upset, Fernando commented.

"This piece of shit doesn't want to start. My guy's supposed to be there at nine. It's already fuckin eight-forty now, and this bitch wants to fuck with me."

While I stood at the van's open window, across the parking lot all the windows from the apartments stared down on us. I felt like the whole world was watching. A wave of panic almost took hold of me. I kept my composure, but I let Fernando know my true feelings.

"Yo, Fernando. Fuck this. Let's just call it off. I've got a bad feeling anyway and the way this van is acting, it's not helping my gut none."

"NO! We're not callin' nothin' off. This is gonna happen today.", Fernando raised his voice, looking at me with a crazed look in his eyes. "Is the Buick running?"

"Yes," I said, feeling like I just wanted to go into the apartment and hide my head under the pillow.

Fernando handed me the walkie-talkie and then got out of the van. I watched as he walked over to the Buick. He got into the driver's seat; I jumped into the driver's seat of the van. I called Charlie on the walkietalkie to inform him as to what was going on. Fernando drove the Buick through the parking lot and pulled it into the spot to the left of the van. I watched as he stepped out of the car and walked around to the trunk. After pulling out a pair of jumper cables, he returned back to the front of the vehicles and opened the hood of the Buick. He hooked the two prongs to the Buick's battery, and then he looked up at me in the van.

"Pop the hood," he ordered. I opened the hood to the van. When Fernando had the other end of the cables connected to the van's battery, he gave more instructions. "Hit the ignition and press the gas once." I did as Fernando instructed and the van started right up. "Okay. We're in business," Fernando called out, pulling the cables and shutting the hood.

I personally wasn't so sure. We had gotten the van started, true. But the last thing we needed after robbing an armored car was to run to a get-a-way car that didn't want to get away. How could we be sure that the van would start up when we really needed it to? When Fernando came back to the driver's side of the van, I got out and gave him back the walkie-talkie. When I sat back in the driver's seat of the Buick, Fernando called me.

"Yo, drive closer to the apartment."

I did as he said. I pulled the car up closer to the apartment door. I could see from where I waited as Fernando spoke into that radio. Just as fast as Fernando set the radio down, Jose and Charlie walked out the door. They both looked balky and out of place. The bag that Charlie carried looked as if it already was packed with a million dollars worth of bills bricked together. They both made their way to their designated vehicle. Charlie ducked into the Buick with me, stuffing the heavy bags between the seats. Jose jumped into the passenger's seat of the van. Fernando pulled the van out in front of me. As he headed towards Route Seventy, Charlie and I followed. I could hear the exchange that Charlie and Jose had over the two way radios.

"Yo," I heard Jose's voice crackle over the radio.

"I hear ya. What's up?" Charlie said.

"We're gonna keep our eyes open for anything out of the ordinary from up here. I'll give ya a heads up if I see anything worth tellin' ya about."

"Sounds good to me," Charlie said. Just as Charlie replied, the street light we approached turned red right before I was able to get through it. I hadn't made it, but Fernando and Jose did, but now we were separated.

"Tell Jose if he plans on looking out for us, he can start by watching these damn lights. I'm not trying to beat the red."

Charlie relayed the message and Jose said they'd pull over and wait.

While I waited for the light to turn green, I watched my side and rear view mirrors. I surveyed our surroundings to be sure we were still okay. I was feeling a little uneasy. Nothing was out of the ordinary, at least, nothing that I could see. There really wasn't much traffic, just a van that pulled up alongside of us as we waited at the light. From the back seat, Charlie's voice, distinct and excited, interrupted my thoughts.

"Yo, that white guy in that van just looked right at me."

I looked over, but the man in the driver's seat didn't seem to be paying us much attention. Without turning my head back to look, I questioned him.

"Are you sure, Charlie? Or are you just being paranoid?"

"I could've sworn he was lookin' dead at me," Charlie said, in an urgent tone.

I continued to watch the van out of the corner of my eye. When the light turned green, the driver of the maroon colored van pulled away as if nothing was for the worse. I held back for just a moment, watching the vehicle as it pulled away.

"What do you want to do?" I asked Charlie, when I finally pulled off.

"Keep going. But if we see that van again, know it's a cop."

I caught up with Jose and Fernando where they were parked along the right side of the street. When they noticed us coming up from their rear, Fernando pulled the van back out onto the road and continued to lead the way.

We finally arrived in Cherry Hill. Fernando pulled off the road into a housing area to park the van. I followed him. As he pulled in front of a house with a picture window that spanned half of the entire front of the home, the window faced out directly at us. I pulled the Buick over across the street a few feet up ahead of Fernando. Suddenly, two alarm bells started ringing in my head.

The first occurred as we slowed down to park, a car passed by us, driving a little too slow for my taste. The driver looked over dressed for a decent September morning like the one we were having. Actually, he looked a lot like we did. He also sat low in his seat. Right then, the whole scene felt wrong.

The second time occurred when it turned out that the house we pulled up in front of wasn't empty. I could see a guy standing on the other side of the glass, looking out at us.

"Yo. There is a guy in that window staring at us." I told Charlie. He raised his head up above the back seat.

"Why the hell did this asshole park us here all wide open like this?"

"I don't know, but here they come." Fernando walked to the driver's side of the Buick, when he opened the door; I slid over across the bench seat so that he could drive the rest of the way. Jose got into the back, behind me, with Charlie.

"There's a guy in that house standing at the window looking right at us." I said to Fernando.

What the fuck, Fernando?" Jose said, "Yeah, man. I see him too, and that shit ain't cool."

"Fernando, we have to call this thing off. Too many things feel out of place. This ain't gonna work," I said.

"I already told you, Joe. We're not callin' anything off. We're ahead of the game. We have scanners, so we can hear if the police are coming. We're way too close right now. I can just smell that cash. I'll be damned if we turn back, hell no. We're gonna make this thing happen."

Fernando pulled away from the house and entered back onto the street. We headed south towards the Walt Whitman Service Plaza, which was only a quarter of a mile ahead of us. Fernando chose that route, because he said there wasn't much traffic at that time of the morning, and most importantly, there were no toll booths. It all made for easy access to the rear service road.

Once we entered onto the rear road, we were on our final stretch. Just on the other end of that small windy road was the entrance of the rear parking lot of the service area. There was no turning back, and I simply didn't like the way anything were feeling. When the main building of the service plaza came into sight, my chest got tight with worry.

I wasn't sure if today was going to be a good day. Entering the front of the parking lot, we followed the black top to our left. A sky blue Crown Victoria rested on the opposite side of the gas pumps. We didn't see it at first, but there it was staring menacingly at us, while we made our way down from the South end of the building. We noticed dark limo tint shaded every window of the car. On the front bumper, white United States Government plates answered any questions we may have had concerning our circumstances.

"Oh shit, it's the Feds," I said, my voice betraying my attempts at staying calm. "Ah, shit. It's about to get ugly."

At that moment, we still did not panic, although we were on the verge. We continued to slowly creep through the parking lot, heading towards the far end, where the lot bordered the large patch of trees. Watching our surroundings intently, we could see that there were few cars lined up in front of the plaza building in various parking spaces. One vehicle stood out on its own. A blue Chevy Suburban sat parked in the middle row of the lot, facing the building. When we passed the SUV, we could see one person. He sat in the driver's seat, faking as if he was reading a newspaper. I could see him staring at his side mirror with his driver's side window down once we passed by him. His shoulders bulged just slightly in a disproportionate manner. The giveaway signs of body armor.

We pulled up at the far end of the parking lot. We turned the car around and backed into one of the parking spaces, which allowed us to see the entire parking area. We sat there, feeling uneasy and contemplating our next move. It was evident that we were not alone at the rest stop. There were no patrons, but the weight of the stares from the unseen eyes that watched us pressured down heavily on our minds. At the bottom left corner of the parking lot, only several spaces away from where we sat, was a lone Winnebago. We could actually see faces peeking out from behind the blinds.

So there we were. Undoubtedly, we were surrounded by cops. Tension was high. We all knew at that point that we were in for trouble, yet, so far, we hadn't committed any crimes. So we couldn't be arrested without committing any crime.

So I thought.

From our position, we had a clear view of everything within the entire parking lot. At the other end of the lot, our friend, the mid-sized tow truck, had made its way to the front and positioned itself along side of the gas pumps. The driver had gotten out, acting as if he were getting gas for his vehicle. Instinctively, we could feel his stare on us. When he re-entered the truck, he just sat there not making any moves. Panic threatened to take over. We knew we had to get the hell out of there and fast.

Nonchalantly, Fernando removed his hat. Suddenly, the tow truck began to move away from the pumps. Seemingly from out of nowhere, a white panel truck appeared. The blue SUV abandoned its post as well. They all approached slowly, bearing down on us. It reminded me of a pride of lioness, moving in for the kill. We had seen enough. We did not tell Fernando, we yelled at him.

"Get us the hell out of here."

Fernando did pull off, but he didn't seem to be in any hurry to go anywhere. With a V-8 motor under the hood of our "borrowed" Buick, not once did the engine rev its RPM's or screech its tires in hurried take off. We took off so slow that men could have effortlessly jogged alongside of us.

"What are you doing," I screamed at Fernando in panic. "Hurry up, Go! Go! Go!"

In a maneuver that escaped our attention, the tow truck managed to make its way behind us and ram the rear of the car, hard. The Buick bucked and we jerked in our seats. I can't be sure of the exact sequence of events. Things got pretty chaotic fast. Was it before or after the Suburban crashed into us in the rear side panel? I don't know for sure. What I am sure of is the first bullet came through the front windshield, striking at an angle. The splintered glass spread in particles all over my hand. From my left, I heard a thud, and the sound of Fernando gasping for air. He has been struck in the chest. The impact brought him huddled crouch, pushing himself as far down below the dash board as his wide frame could get.

Fortunately, Fernando had opted to wear his bulletproof vest that morning. The impact of the bullet didn't kill him, but he definitely suffered a serious bruise. Still, Fernando never bothered to accelerate or try to speed us out of there. We just drifted in slow motion. From our left, I could see ten men dressed in all black and S.W.A.T. gear charging at us in full sprint, machine guns at ready.

When I looked back to where the Winnebago was parked, I could see more people piling out of the motor home. All of them were armed to the teeth. They were dressed differently from the S.W.A.T. guys. They looked like vigilantes dressed in civilian clothes hell bent for revenge. From our left, the first on coming S.W.A.T. team opened fire. They riddled the car with semi-automatic gun fire. Still tucked under the dash board, Fernando finally decided to give the car a little gas. He drove past the first cluster of flying bullets, attempting to round the corner that led back to the rear of the main building.

Driving toward the turn off, we were again assaulted from the rear by the tow truck. This time it got us on our rear side panel, literally rolling the end of the car. The impact from the tow truck crushed the entire rear panel. The wheel well caved in, crushing the tire in place. We were moored; dead in water, so to speak. The car was going nowhere. Fernando threw the car in park and fled. He ran straight and laid himself face down. His arms and legs were spread out to surrender.

Fernando was never instructed by anyone to get out of the car, so I thought at the time. My cousin just chose his own course of action. As for myself, I was fixed on getting the hell out of dodge. When Fernando made a break for it, so did I. My door popped open without any problem and I fell to the ground, using the car as a shield. I was a bit weighed down. My hands were empty, but I wore tight black driving gloves. I wore a bullet proof vest. Over top of the vest, I had on a tactical vest loaded with ammunition that clung to my body. A hand held scanner device sat in a case snapped to my waist right next to my diver's knife. All that gear definitely added weight. But I hardly noticed. Obviously, I was more interested in not getting shot. As far as I was concerned, the car already suffered considerable enough damage for all of us. I just wanted to get as far away as possible.

I ran to the front of the main building, ducking my head as projectiles flew past me. I headed for the double doors of a store. Bullets whistled passed my head, ricocheting and spraying particles of rock and cinder as they impacted the wall of the building. I dipped my head below my shoulders as low as I could, as if that would actually protect me from flying bullets. The airborne projectiles bouncing off the walls forced me to divert my course. I headed up the sidewalk to a door. When I reached for the handle, glass shattered all over me and around me from the continued gunfire.

I turned away from the door and ran towards the top end of the main building, hoping to keep myself from being shot. When I turned the comer, I headed straight for the Coca-Cola machine that was placed up against the side wall of the building. Tiny missiles of death were flying recklessly through the air. I had to take whatever cover I could find. I felt like a damn pinball bouncing around, trying to dodge all those bullets. I ran along the side of the wall, hoping that by keeping the soda machine between me and my pursuers, I could avoid injury and make my escape. With the rear corner of the building just several steps away, my leg suddenly went limp and gave out. It stopped working completely, causing me to crash to the ground, as if I had stepped into a large hole.

This is going to sound corny, but it's true.

Everything fell quiet as I laid there on the ground. It was like I had completely lost my hearing. I lost all feeling through my body and blackness blotted out my sight. In my mind's eye, I could see the warm gentle smile on the face of the woman I love. In that brief moment of serenity, I knew I had made the biggest mistake of my life. Reality slowly phased back into focus through the cracks of my semi-consciousness. The sound of gun fire returned my mind to the real world, making me acutely aware that my boy Jose and my brother Charlie were still being fired upon. I attempted to lift myself up, but the searing pain in my thigh kept me planted on the ground. I had been hit, and I was not going anywhere. I laid there wounded. I could see from where I had fallen the car that I had fled from.

Jose was trying to push the rear door open while the federal S.W.A.T. team Swiss cheesed the vehicle. My brother was on the other side of Jose in the back seat. The rear doors had been jammed shut when the tow truck barreled over the back side of the Buick.

They were trapped.

I could see them both trying to raise their hands in surrender, but the police continued to fire, ignoring them. They were forced to take cover between the seats of the car under siege. It was clear that Charlie and Jose had no intentions of returning fire. After three attempts of them trying to prove just that, I finally heard a voice holler out.

"Put your hands up!

Of course, Jose and Charlie had already been trying to do that. For some reason, the firing squad wasn't quite satisfied with that approach at first. I guess after launching countless numbers projectiles, most of which hit the building or caused a dangerous cross fire between the authorities, they had no choice but to finally relent. Laying there watching the assault on my brother and Jose finally wind down to an end, I heard footsteps hurrying towards me. Part of the assault team had made its way to where I laid wounded.

Although I was already laid out on my face, I heard an angry voice say, "Get Down! Get the fuck down. I'll blow your fucking head off."

I turned my head away from my brother and Soto just as they exited the car to give themselves up. I looked around to see the officers that surrounded me. Exhausted and defeated, all I could see were the barrels of multiple guns pointed at my head.

The S.W.A.T. guys pounced on me, and then flopped me over on my back. All the equipment I had strapped to my body made it difficult for them to cuff me. They wanted to be sure that I didn't get a chance to somehow get a shot off with my gun that was holstered to my waist. Not that I would've been stupid enough to make any kind of move with all that fire power just inches from my face. Hell, I didn't even want to sneeze.

The S. W.A.T. members crushed me as they placed their knees down on the back of my neck. Their weight had damn near pressed all the air out of my lungs. In a wheezy voice, I managed to say, "I'm hit. I'm hit."

"Where?" and officer asked.

I told them that my thigh hurt. They quickly rolled me onto my back and unzipped my vest. They relived me of all my gear. My tactical vest, my bullet proof vest, my gloves, my scanner and of course my gun, were all taken. The medical examiner on hand had the S.W.A.T. boys roll me onto my side so that he could check my wound. He lowered my pants beneath my waist just enough to see the entry point.

"Alright," he said, and the S.W.A.T. guys rolled me back on to my stomach. They made sure the cuffs were on good and secure.

After being sure that I was no longer an immediate threat, they threw me into the back of an ambulance, and I was carted away. I was later informed that I had been fortunate. The bullet had actually struck the gun that was bolstered to my hip and fragmented. The fragments were what ultimately caused the wound. There was no major leakage and no severe damage. When it happened, the furthest thought from my mind was that the bullet fragmented. All I knew was that I was hit, and it hurt like hell.

I was immediately taken to the hospital. The doctor didn't spend that much time on me. He x-rayed my wound, cleaned out all the metal fragments and quickly bandaged me up. About twenty minutes later, I was taken from the hospital and transported directly to the federal court house. I was placed in a holding cell by myself. I may have been by myself in the cell, but I wasn't by myself on the floor that housed the holding cells. I couldn't see my brother and Jose, but I could holler to them through the bars of my cell.

The feds had placed us on the same floor of the building; however, we were just placed in different holding cells, which were also divided by walls made of cinder blocks. I was relieved to hear my brother's voice and to know that he was okay. I felt the same about my friend Jose.

At about eleven o'clock that morning, one-by-one, we were taken to the court room for arraignment. My cousin Fernando was nowhere to be seen.

8:46 PM Interior of the stolen Buick. The duffle bags were found closed like shown here. Yet authorities listed all the guns in the complaint by 11:00 A.M. The state police were the ones to remove the guns and bags from car after 8:00 P.M. on 9-1-98. 9-1-98 - These photos show the time our weapons were removed from the car.

8:51 PM. These are the duffle bags found inside the Buick. The time,
9:00 PM. that's written on the bag, conflicts with the time
the actual criminal complaint with the detailed inventory
log filed that same morning before the magistrate judge.

Aerial views of the Walt Whitman Service Plaza
in Cherry Hill, New Jersey.

Fernando Flores.

Our car on 9/1/98. It was stolen.

Chapter 31
Summary of the Setup

F ernando Flores was born on the island of Puerto Rico, on December 9, 1972. While still a young boy, his parents moved from the island all the way to Camden County, New Jersey. Growing up, Fernando's life was typical of those who were raised inside an urban neighborhood. A usual teenager, Fernando learned his way around the streets of Camden.

At a young age, Fernando developed a taste for guns. By the time he'd reached fourteen, he was arrested for bringing a gun into a school in Pine Poynt's School District. In juvenile court, he was convicted and sentenced to serve one year at Lakeland Juvenile Complex. (1) Unfortunately, that arrest and conviction was only the beginning of his journey down mishap lane. Shortly after his release from Lakeland, Fernando was again arrested. At the age of sixteen, he was charged and convicted of, a drug offense that occurred at his parent's. (2)

Fernando's arrests didn't end there. He faced several juvenile charges, mainly from dealing petty drugs. However, his lifestyle on the streets progressed. He began to supplement his income from small odd jobs to buying and selling guns illegally. From time to time, he found himself on the street corners of Camden pushing drugs. As Fernando grew more and more into himself, his appetite for guns became insatiable. In an interview with Jerry Wright, an investigator for the Federal Public Defender's Office, Marissa Rivera, sister to Joseph and Charlie Rodriguez, described Fernando as being, "a gun freak." She stated that, "with Fernando, the bigger the gun, the better." (3)

While growing up, in order to support himself, Fernando worked odd jobs and engaged in shady deals that were done under the table. He'd always enjoyed partying and chasing women. His biggest addiction, developed as a budding twin to his gun obsession, which was money. Sadly, as a youth, it was never a big issue for Fernando to take any kind of risk to obtain his goals, and in adulthood, not much had changed.

In an interview with Jean Louis Adams, Investigator for the Federal Public Defender's Office, Brenda Bennet referred to Fernando's behavior as, "under handed and crooked." (4)

Brenda Bennet met Fernando Flores sometime between the year of 1990 and 1991. She had been at a party in Palmyra, New Jersey when she acquainted herself with him for the first time. From that night forward, Brenda became Fernando's official girlfriend. Although Brenda was a married woman at the time, Fernando "quickly took her away from her husband." (5) It was only a matter of months before the two had moved into an apartment together as well. In time, Brenda realized that she had fallen in love with a monster. In time, she became the mother of two of his children. Through multiple experiences, she would also learn how abusive Fernando could be. She suffered verbal, mental, emotional, and even physical abuse as a result of living with Fernando. Unfortunately, just like with any other dysfunctional relationship, Brenda continued to stay with Fernando. She even supported him in many of ideas, and without ever questioning him, she took whatever he dished out and continued to care for their two children.

Fernando's educational skills were limited, too. Without a high school diploma or a G.E.D., he was hard pressed to find a good job. When he and Brenda first met, he was selling drugs and working through a temporary service. (6) Finally, Fernando did find himself a job working for a company called, Sportsmen's Loft. It was a gun shop and shooting range. The perfect combination for Fernando's gun obsessed mind.

It was there, at the Loft, that Fernando would meet the man who would later become a close friend. Roy Whitmore, a Sergeant with the New Jersey, Merchantville Police Department grew close to Fernando. The two often discussed guns while they took advantage of the shooting range together. Between the years of 1994 and 1995, Roy Whitmore put the idea in motion for Fernando to apply to be a police officer for the Merchantville Police Department.

First, Fernando needed to apply to the Police Academy. Without his G.E.D. or high school diploma, Fernando was faced with a dilemma. He could come clean with the academy and admit that he didn't have either of the requirements to proceed with the academy's program, or he could forget the whole thing. Walking away wasn't an option for him, and obtaining a G.E.D. would take too much time. So, Fernando tried to persuade his sister to allow him to make a bogus copy of her G.E.D certificate, with his name in place of hers.

Initially, she agreed, but an argument between the two turned his sister against him, so in the end, she refused to go through with it and Fernando was still without a G.E.D. Undeterred, Fernando proceeded with his interview at the academy as scheduled. Fortunately for him, the academy never checked into his educational background. With Sergeant Whitmore's endorsement, and being sponsored by the Merchantville Police Department, Fernando was accepted into the academy. (7) Shortly after the completion of the academy's program, Fernando was officially hired as a Merchantville Police Officer.

Fernando may have entered into a respectable profession, but his flawed personality followed, and as a result, his time as a police officer was plagued with problems. His career was short lived, and during his two years on the force, numerous complaints were lodged against him.

Brenda Bennet stated that, "Fernando abused his power, abusing people, issuing unjustifiable tickets and stealing police property for his own use." (8) Fernando became increasingly violent and obsessed; therefore, he "would do anything for money and power." (9)

In 1996, just within two years of being employed as a police officer, Fernando's violent temper highlighted the turning point in his career. In a fit of rage, he hit Brenda, pointed a gun at her head and threatened to kill her. Following the incident, Brenda filed for a temporary restraining order against him for domestic violence. (10) Being a police officer, the Domestic Violence Report prompted an immediate investigation into Fernando's behavior, especially since the report was filed with his own department. Of course, by law, they had to confiscate all his weapons. (11)

During this time, it was learned that Fernando was in possession of a firearm that had been missing from the police evidence locker. Fernando's two years on the force were rocky at best, but even when it was clear that Fernando could no longer wear a badge, the Blue Wall still held strong. It was apparent that Fernando had problems, yet he was still a fellow officer. Therefore, instead of being officially fired from the Police Department, they kind of put it as he was, "forced to resign." (12) Fernando was devastated when he lost his job as a police officer. His mood became sour and his deposition a little meaner. I guess that is because all he ever wanted to be was a police officer. (13)

After the abrupt ending of his police career, Fernando was again forced to find work at a more menial place of employment. He eventually landed a part-time position, working as a manager at a paintball store in a Columbus flea market. He also found part-time work with a refrigeration and air conditioning company in Mount Laurel, New Jersey. Fernando clearly wasn't happy with either of his two jobs, and he wanted to find a way back into law enforcement. Unfortunately for him, his history with the Merchantville Police Department, made finding work as a cop in another district unlikely.

It is said, "Every dog has his day", and in the summer of 1998, Fernando's day had come. Fernando's long time friend and fellow officer at the Merchantville Police Department, Sergeant Roy Whitmore, approached him with some important news. Whitmore informed Fernando that someone from the Federal Bureau of Investigation (F.B.I.) was interested in speaking with him. (14) Fernando agreed to a meeting, with Sergeant Whitmore as the go between, Special Agent John Tamm and Fernando Flores became acquainted with each other for the first time. S.A. Tamm knew Fernando and Charlie Rodriguez were first cousins, which is why the F.B.I, wanted to speak with him in the first place. They wanted Charlie Rodriguez, and they wanted Fernando to help.

Fernando would have done anything to get back on the force, (15) so when the F.B.I, offered Fernando approximately forty thousand dollars and a reinstated position as a police officer in the state of Florida, he never hesitated to become an informant against his own cousin. During the investigation of the February 12, 1997, shooting of Officer Steven Leoni III, the authorities apprehended a suspect by the name of Jose Baez. Baez was an acquaintance of Charlie Rodriguez. He eventually gave the authorities Charlie's name as the shooter. Baez gave several varied statements of what supposedly happened on that night. His statements turned out to be less then credible, but it was irrelevant at that time. With the abandoned car used in the shooting being in the name of Charlie's girlfriend and Baez throwing his name around like a softball, it was inevitable that Charlie be named the prime suspect in the shooting of the officer.

An arrest warrant was issued immediately, and for fear of his own safety, as well as from prosecution, Charlie Rodriguez fled. He became one of America's Most Wanted fugitives. He was dubbed, "Crazy Charlie" by the media. He remained underground, while authorities repeatedly harassed friends and family, trying to learn his whereabouts. For the authorities, the hunt for Charlie was personal. He was accused of shooting one of their own. The contempt for Charlie became evident when the law raided a home in Camden, thinking Charlie was there. The kid they located ended up in the hospital because they believed he was Charlie Rodriguez. They beat this kid, broke his leg and just tore him up for nothing." (16)

During the time Charlie was on the run, I, Joseph Rodriguez became the focus of the state and federal officials. I was continuously followed daily. Authorities maintained a watchful eye, and I was even openly confronted by a team of detectives that had been watching me. The verbal confrontation with those officers left me a bit unnerved, but still, there was nothing I could do for them. I really didn't know where Charlie was.

By putting pressure on me, the F.B.I, hoped to find a lead on Charlie, but their efforts gained them nothing. All the surveillance and tails led nowhere. The Feds knew that they needed to find another way to lure Charlie out of hiding. The authorities knew "... to get to Charlie, the F.B.I had to get to me."(17) And that's where Fernando Flores entered the picture. It was his job to use his family relationship to befriend me in order to coax me for information on Charlie's location. The question became how he would go about doing it. While Fernando worked on building Joseph's trust, he maintained constant contact with Special Agent John Tamm. After several weeks of discreet meetings with the F.B.I., Fernando was instructed to convince me to agree to take part in a robbery of what would be a nonexistent armored truck. Special Agent Tamm was the brainchild of the armored truck plan. The idea was that Fernando's friend worked for the armored car service, but was heavy in gambling debts. The friend was desperate and willing to give up inside information. The location of the robbery was to be at the Walt Whitman Service Plaza in Cherry Hill on the New Jersey Turnpike.

Fernando was fully instructed as to what his mission was. There was much to gain for his part if he was to succeed. Fernando was determined to play his role and bring down me and my brother. From out of nowhere, Fernando latched on to me and was so persistent about getting close to me.... It was awfully coincidental that after all of the years of my family living in Camden that Fernando just out of nowhere decides to get close to me. In fact, it was very odd for me and my brother Charlie to even hang with Fernando at all, so I should have followed my gut. (18)

In the weeks preceding the September 1, 1998 incident, Fernando Flores was steadily determined in his efforts to persuade me into agreeing to take part in the robbery. He pushed and pushed this armored car thing on me. I said no a hundred times. I even agreed once, and then stood him up on the day it was supposed to initially happen. But he just wouldn't give up. I really thought he was just that desperate. And a million dollars is what he used to entice me. A million dollars is a nice chunk of change. That would be hard for anybody to resist. We weren't rich people, and my brother needed a good lawyer to help him out with his legal issues, regarding the shooting of Officer Leoni," I said during an interview.

The F.B.I didn't seem to be content with simply setting Charlie up to take the fall for a phony robbery scenario. They wanted to be sure Charlie Rodriguez was buried under the jail. Between the years of 1997-1998, forty-one banks were victimized by armed men in mask. With no leads on many of the bank robberies, the F.B.I. intended to attach Charlie's name to several of those unsolved robberies. Unfortunately, for anyone caught with Charlie, they too, would become suspects in the bank robberies, simply so the Feds had someone to prosecute. In fact, the forty thousand dollars offered to Fernando for his involvement with our setup was not a government reward. The money was offered up by the Commerce Bank, one of the victims of the many unsolved robberies. The F.B.I, viewed the Charlie Rodriguez situation as a perfect opportunity. Fernando would make the perfect informant. Lure Charlie into a false robbery, collar him or worse.

Then after the smoke cleared, file charges of armed bank robbery using Fernando as their "witness." Yeah, they had it all planned out, because they were going to blame the Commerce Bank robberies on Charlie...(19)

The Feds knew what they wanted. And they had no problems playing dirty. What better fall guy than the man wanted for shooting a police officer? For the F.B.I., it was a great production and Fernando Flores was their poster boy. He had allowed the government to fully infiltrate his life. The F.B.I.'s discreet presence didn't sway Brenda Bennet. She noticed holes drilled in her bathroom ceiling-holes that she was positive were not there before. (20)

Prior to the September 1st incident, Brenda recognized Fernando's strange behavior. I knew something shady was going on, but I didn't know what. (21) Fernando became erratic, evasive and more irritated with his live in girlfriend. At odd hours, he would force Brenda to leave the house. One evening, Jose Soto and I showed up at the apartment door looking for Fernando. Brenda informed us that Fernando wasn't home. As we were leaving, Jose and I began walking through the parking to the car. There, we met up with Fernando and returned to his apartment. Brenda had been sick that night, so she was already dressed in her pajamas. "Fernando comes in the bedroom, gives me money, ask if I would go to the supermarket to pick up some ham and cheese. He gives me a list of things he wanted. But basically, he just wanted me out of the way. (22)

As part of the elaborate setup, Fernando complimented my psyche by initiating conversation about subjects even I could relate to. "Guns." With me being on parole, I was unable to be around firearms. Still, Fernando tried numerous times to sell me pistols, without any success. Fernando had even been consistent about learning Charlie's location. Naturally, I was withdrawn and guarded on the subject of my brother. The F.B.I had pressured Fernando for more information on Charlie, so he continued to persist in trying to gain information from me. The idea of the armored car robbery, which Fernando claimed would, "Help Charlie," I knew could also turn out to do just the opposite.

I knew that my brother had a long legal battle ahead him, and that attorney fees would cripple our family. Our natural fear was that a Public Defender would not have Charlie's best interest at heart, and that plagued me and my brother's mind. So eventually, I put word out on the streets that I needed to speak to Charlie. After a little more than a week, I was confronted by an unknown man in front of my own home. The man handed me a brown paper bag that contained one walkie-talkie radio and a charger.

The radio's frequency was already pre-set to contact Charlie, and by letting my cousin talk to him, I'd hoped to end Fernando's incessant persistence about the armored car robbery after hearing Charlie say, no. Unfortunately, no thanks to Fernando, by the time all was said and done, Charlie was drawn into Fernando's madness.

The F.B.I, was going to do what they could to charge Charlie with those bank robberies. And Fernando clearly aware listening devices had been installed throughout his apartment, continuously get me caught up. Get this, "...Fernando had advised Brenda not to say too much over the phone." (23) The plan was to get Charlie on tape admitting to one or more of the bank robberies. Yet, during the interview with Marissa Rivera, the Private Investigator, Jerry Wright learned Brenda Bennet had expressed to Marissa that, "... Charlie told Fernando on tape that he did not commit the robberies."(24) The audio tapes produced nothing, but the jury at trial would never learn about the audio surveillance. Nor would they ever be made aware of the fact that I, Joseph

Rodriguez was under visual surveillance while me and my brother supposedly robbed banks.

Jose Soto was drawn into the madness simply because he was my friend. Perfect example of wrong place at the wrong time, however, in a reckless attempt to included Jose in the plan; Fernando discussed the plan with me in front of an unsuspecting Soto. Although Soto initially walked away from the proposition, he too, eventually relented.

CHAPTER 32

The Federal Bureau of Investigation was the driving force behind the entire set-up. They had a score to settle, and they were determined to put an end to the whole Charlie Rodriguez ordeal. Nothing was sacred. They wanted Charlie so bad that not only did they create the phony armored car scenario, but they also provided Fernando Flores with his own small arsenal in which to facilitate the fake robbery.

One evening, just days before the armored car robbery was to take place, Fernando entered his Merchantville home carrying a large black duffle bag. Brenda Bennet, entered the living room from the hallway leading from the bedroom. Surprisingly, she walked in on Fernando just in time to witness him putting a bag into the closet. She said, "… he told me 'Don't go in the closet. Do you understand'". (25)

Brenda's curiosity got the best of her. The moment Fernando left the apartment, she took the opportunity to look inside the bag and reported that she noticed, "There were semiautomatic weapons and bullet proof vests in there." (26) Brenda always knew Fernando to have an obsession with guns, but she was stunned nonetheless, and nervous. The caliber and amount of weaponry took her by surprise. And with all the shadiness that she had witnessed from Fernando, she feared that this particular bag had a purpose, expressing that "... he admitted to me after it was all over that those weapons were supplied by the F.B.I." (27)

The F.B.I actually put operable weapons with live ammunition onto the streets in order to facilitate a phony robbery. But the weapons were not provided simply to make the robbery attempt look good, they served another purpose, "... they wanted us dead."(28)

The F.B.I, reasoned that if the suspects were well armed, there would be cause to open fire and end the Rodriguez fiasco once and for all. The Walt Whitman Service Plaza scenario was an orchestrated assassination attempt, "...if they wanted to, they could have taken the brothers down on several occasions prior to the rest stop." (29) The idea was to justify the shooting and killing of the suspects by showing an array of firepower seized from the car. After their deaths, there would not be a trial, and no one to contest the setup at the service plaza or the bank robbery allegations.

But my brother, Jose Soto and I did survive. On the morning of September 1, 1998, Brenda Bennet described Fernando's behavior as, "abnormal" and "weird". She explained that during that time, she was working from six-thirty A.M. to four-thirty P.M., Monday through Friday. Each morning she would prepare herself for work, pack up her children, and leave the apartment by five-thirty A.M. to drop the children off at Fernando's mother's house. She then needed to make it to Morristown, New Jersey by six-thirty A.M. in order to be at work on time. (30)

That particular morning, Fernando rushed her out of the house much earlier than she would normally leave. His behavior was noticeably unusual. At four-fifty in the morning, before she was fully ready for work, Fernando pressured her to leave by saying that it was time to go. He rushed her out of the apartment door, and walked her and the children to the car. He watched as they drove away. That, Brenda admitted, was something that Fernando had never done in all the years she spent with him. (31)

Shortly after Brenda's early departure, Jose and my brother and I entered into the apartment. Inside, Joseph, Charlie and Jose learned about the canvas bag full of weapons for the first time. "It was like this guy was geared for war. I couldn't believe all the shit he had. There was a J-15 automatic rifle, a damn Mac.-1 1 auto machine gun with a silencer. Hell, this guy even had an assortment of hand guns. He pulled out a vest for each of us; bulletproof and utility vests. Fernando also provided us with small disguises like wigs and stuff. The guy was geared up to his neck with equipment." (32)

Being that it was so early in the morning, we complained of being hungry. Fernando admitted that he offered to go out and get food, he stated, "…when I went to the 7-Eleven to go buy orange juice,"(33) Fernando contacted the F.B.I, once the opportunity presented itself. Without any doubts, the F.B.I. knew that a wanted fugitive was within easy reach. Fernando had been sure to keep them informed. A known fugitive was held up in an apartment with no way to escape, yet the F.B.I, never made any attempt to apprehend him at the apartment.

For this lack of diligence, the F.B.I, explained that, "they didn't want to risk a shootout in a residential neighborhood. "(34) The F.B.I was aware of the amount of weaponry that was being held in the apartment, because they were the ones who supplied them. Still, the F.B.I.'s reasoning for not taking Charlie into custody, while he was at the apartment was without merit, "They could've taken them down at my apartment, because it wasn't until about an hour and a half, maybe two hours, after they were there that they started to load the weapons. "(35)

The F.B.I was fully aware that the weapons weren't yet loaded at the time Fernando used his absence from the apartment to contact them. Yet they did nothing. The F.B.I, allowed the scenario to play out, including letting three armed men with automatic weapons, one a known wanted fugitive, to drive through the streets of New Jersey. Of course, the F.B.I had ulterior motives for allowing wanted fugitive, Charlie Rodriguez, to continue on to his predetermined destination. Jose and the Rodriguez brothers were unaware of what awaited them at the Walt Whitman Service area that September 1, 1998 morning.

A tactical assassination team of Federal agents lay in wait for the crew to arrive, "the plan was for the three to get killed in the incident... that Fernando was to flee the scene of the gunfire." (36) As far as the F.B.I, was concerned, "...the deader, the better,"(37) speaking of Soto and my brother and I. While at the rest stop, Fernando, who was at the wheel of the Buick, drove the small crew into the F.B.I's trap. Realizing something was wrong, Charlie urged Fernando to pull away and drive out of the rest area. Fernando barely pressed his foot on the accelerator, presenting no challenge to the looming agents waiting.

Fernando slowly crept through the service area's front parking lot. The agents, seeing easy prey, opened fire on the Buick. Without justifiable provocation, from my stand point, the federal agents launched a barrage of bullets into the stolen vehicle.

A tow-truck, driven by an agent, rammed into the rear of the Buick. The impact was so severe, that the rear panels of the car were buckled, which jammed the rear doors shut. The buckled doors also pinned Jose Soto and Charlie Rodriguez in the back seat. The rear wheel had been crushed in, disabling the Buick. Trapped in the back seat, Jose and Charlie ducked as low as possible, trying to stay out of the way of the bullets, as the agents assaulted the vehicle with heavy gunfire.

I did manage to get out of the passenger door, as gunfire came from my far left, and right. I hoped to find some cover inside the building of the rest stop, which is why I ran alongside the building, ducking and trying to dodge the flying projectiles that were seeking their mark.

Fernando had a difficult time of his own, "...the plan had not gone as drawn up... someone rolled up onto the car and Fernando couldn't get out." (38) Taking a bullet in the chest, Fernando crouched down as low as he could to avoid being shot again. He continued to kick at the door until it finally opened. When he finally opened the door, he laid himself down at the agent's feet to surrender. Had it not been for the bulletproof vest, Fernando would've died that day.

F.B.I, Agents and S.W.A.T. continued to fire upon the Buick. Jose Soto and my brother Charlie Rodriguez were trapped in the back seat, attempting to raise their hands several times to surrender. Their attempts were only met by more relentless gunfire.

When the shooting finally stopped, shell casings and glass debris littered the rest area. It was a miracle that no one was killed. Jose sustained no injuries. A bullet grazed Charlie's thigh. I was injured in the hip by a fragmented projectile and Fernando suffered a bruised chest. One of the officers was cut by flying glass shards that scattered about by the gunfire.

Jose Soto and my brother and I were initially charged with that officer's injuries, but the charge was dropped, because the circumstances surrounding the shooting were deemed unclear. We were each cuffed and officially arrested. Soto and Charlie were eventually transported to the County Federal Courthouse, while I was carted away in an ambulance and taken to the hospital to be treated for a minor gunshot wound. Later that morning, I joined Soto and my brother at the court house.

The Walt Whitman Service Plaza incident dominated the news. Every major broadcast station aired the capture of one of America's Most Wanted fugitives. Marissa Rivera, my sister, learned of the arrest of her two brothers, while working at the Mediplex Rehab Center in Camden. When she heard the news broadcasted, she was in a patient's room, and just so happened to see it on his television. Shortly after the news report, Marissa received a phone call from Luz Flores, Fernando's mother. It wasn't until Luz informed Marissa that Fernando was involved that she realized something major happened.

Brenda Bennet was also at work when she received the news. Fernando's sister, Louisa, called Brenda, asking her to leave work and go to Luz's house. Louisa only explained that something happened to Fernando.

"After everything went down and I got a phone call at work that Fernando was shot, I had to leave. It was a mess. And I had left work. I was a nervous wreck. I went to my mother-in-law's house. Everybody was all crying, upset and I didn't know what was going on," (39) Brenda said.

After what seemed like a lifetime of worry, Fernando himself called his mother's house, Brenda reported that, "He asked to speak with me on the phone and told me to go into the back of the kitchen, away from everybody, he said, 'Listen, I'm okay and we're going to be okay.' I said, what are you talking about? He said, 'We'll talk later. You just calm down and be there for my mom right now. Don't tell anybody what I just told you.'"(40)

Brenda knew better than to question Fernando when his word was final. She had learned the hard way, and knew if she was too pushy about getting information or didn't listen to Fernando, "He would beat the crap out of me again," she confirmed. (41) Brenda did as she was told. She provided emotional support for Fernando's mother and awaited further instructions from Fernando. When he did call his mother's house again, Fernando instructed Brenda to return to their apartment in Merchantville to finish packing for their pre-planned trip to Florida. My birthday happens to be September 5. Suddenly, out of the blue, in August he said, 'For your birthday we're going to go to Disney World. We're going to Florida and you can see your parents.' And I was like something is not right here, because this is not like him. But I figured well, maybe he's changing, because he's acting weird or maybe he's just wiggin' out on me or something." (42)

Brenda would later learn that the pre-planned trip to Florida was nothing more than a cover devised by the F.B.I, in order to get Fernando out of town for a few days after the completion of the operation. It struck Brenda as strange when Fernando called the house soon after the Walt Whitman rest area incident. She found it even more disturbing that he had been able to call numerous times, "I just found it strange that he could make so many calls. I'm sure that, when you do something wrong, you're only allowed one phone call. Well, he called his mom's about four times..." (43)

Nonetheless, confused and scared, Brenda returned home as Fernando instructed. When she arrived at the apartment, she found juice bottles and coffee cake boxes on her kitchen table. It was as if people had been sitting their sometime that morning. It was odd. She knew that no one had been there that morning when she left, but it dawned on her that Fernando's strange behavior that morning may have had something to do with the mess on her table.

Not knowing what else to do, Brenda cleaned up and sat in an empty apartment waiting for Fernando.

A short while later, Fernando made it home. He explained to Brenda that he had been bailed out of jail. But Brenda wasn't buying it. She was panicked and upset. She insisted that he tell her what happened. Fernando only responded by telling her not to worry about it, that he would explain everything later. With all her questions still unanswered, Brenda and Fernando packed up their little family and left New Jersey. It would be a week before they would return. A month passed before Fernando finally admitted to Brenda that he was part of the government's plan to setup his cousins. Fernando explained to Brenda that Charlie, Joseph and Jose Soto were all supposed to get killed. Brenda was stunned that Fernando could knowingly set up his cousins to be executed.

Fernando may have been working for the F.B.I, as in informant, but his own behavior was borderline criminal. While his cousins sat in jail awaiting trial, Fernando was in the free world making Brenda's life a living hell. Brenda, knowing the truth, became a threat to Fernando, at least in his mind. His anger and frustration over what he had done festered inside of him, and he projected those emotions out on Brenda.

Daily, his abuse towards her intensified; and Fernando beat Brenda on several occasions. Brenda filed a restraining order against him, but he ignored it. One night, Fernando searched for Brenda. Once he found her, he beat her up again with the restraining order in effect. Fernando was never officially arrested for the assault, and nothing ever came of the criminal complaint filed by Brenda.

On January 19, 1999, Jean Louis Adams, Senior Private Investigator for the Federal Public Defender's office, with Jackilyn Web, met Brenda Bennet outside of her work place to question her about Fernando. This initial meeting would ultimately spark a seemingly unending feud between Brenda and Fernando. The two investigators were there on behalf of Lisa C. Evans, Public Defender for Jose Soto. Their goal was to learn what they could about Fernando's involvement in the attempted armored car robbery. But their presence outside her work place made Brenda nervous. By the time the investigators arrived at her job, Brenda was aware of what Fernando had done. If she said anything, she was afraid of what might happen. "If Fernando was willing to set his own family up to be executed, she could only imagine what he would do to her." (45)

When Fernando first learned that the investigators had been to talk to Brenda, he let it be known how he felt. That same evening, Fernando called the Investigator's office. He left a message for Jean Louis Adams to contact him. When Jean returned to her office, Investigator Jerry Wright relayed Fernando's message. Attaching a recording device to her phone, she immediately returned Fernando's phone call. After three rings, Fernando answered the phone.

Recorded phone call of Fernando Flores-1/19/99 @ 5:20P.M.
A. Hello?
Q. Hi, is Mr. Flores there?
A. Yeah, who's this?

Q. Hi, Mr. Flores my name is Jean Louis Adams, I just got
   back to the office and Jerry Wright left me a message
A. Right, right.
Q. That you called for me.
A. Yeah.
Q. I, I just spoke with Brenda.
A. Yeah, well, she, I mean why, why you asking all these
   questions; you come and ask me.
Q. Ok. Is it alright if I ask you then?
A. You gonna pay me for my time? Nah, Nah, you ain't
   gonna talk shit over the phone, you gonna pay me for
   my time?
Q. Pay you for...
A. My time is very valuable to me, you gonna pay me for
   my time? Q. Ok. How much would you like me to pay
   you for your time? A. I don't know 200 bucks an hour.
   How's that sound?
Q. $200 an hour?
A. Yup, and I'm very slow.
Q. Well, I have to find out and I have to get the money
   from the Federal Defender's office...
A. Well, if you ain't the big chief then I'm talking to the
   wrong person.

This is investigator Jean Louis Adams, today's date is
Tuesday, January 19, 1999. The time is now 5:20P.M.
throughout the pre-trial investigation, Fernando beat
Brenda Bennet on numerous occasions, ultimately running
her out of New Jersey. After all the fights and restraining
orders, the most disturbing account Brenda remembers,
"I was driving down route 38 coming home from work
and went to press on my breaks and it was like the brakes
wouldn't work, and I slammed into someone's car... Fer-

nando used to do breaks for a living for awhile...God is my witness, in my heart, I know he did it, but I don't have any proof." (46)

Brenda swears that Fernando tampered with her brakes in order to have her killed. Brenda speaking to the defense investigators sparked a fury inside Fernando. It also set the F.B.I, agents in motion, "...Agents Jim Walsh and Peter Loscalzo of the F.B.I, came to see her at work... They told her that they did not like that she and Marissa were friends... Brenda told the F.B.I. that she was scared of Fernando... that she was afraid that Fernando would 'eliminate' her. She also informed them that Fernando had attacked her. They responded that they couldn't get involved in Fernando's personal life." (47)

It all became too much for Brenda Bennet, and in March of 1999, she was finally forced out of New Jersey, "Fernando, and some agents working with him. They were constantly following me. The F.B.I. came to my job, Fernando harassed me at my job. I was forced to resign from my job. They made my life a living hell." (48)

The defense tried to have something done about the harassment. There was an emergency injunction filed, but nothing ever came of it: Fernando, Sergeant Whitmore, and a couple of Fernando's friends all "helped" pack and load Brenda's belongings into the back of a truck. She was sent down to Florida to stay with her parents.

The jury would never get to hear about the other side of Fernando Flores.

CHAPTER 33

In the view of the authorities, my brother and I were notorious throughout the Camden area. We had been suspected of numerous illegal acts, most notably home invasions, yet there was never evidence enough to substantiate an indictment. Charlie Rodriguez was accused of shooting a police officer, making him public enemy number one, because the authorities wanted Charlie, there was no boundaries in their pursuit of him. All they wanted to do was bring him down at all costs. And that's exactly what they did.

On September 1, 1998, I, Joseph Rodriguez was transported to the Camden County Courthouse after being medically treated for an injury. Again, while the shots were fired by F.B.I, and S.W.A.T. agents, Joseph was struck by a bullet. Fortunately, the bullet struck the gun that was strapped to my waist by the holster. It fragmented, making my wound miner and superficial.

Upon arrival at the courthouse, I was placed in a holding cell by myself. Although I was alone in my cell, I was not alone. The floor in the courthouse where holding cells were located was divided by cinder block walls. The cells all connected, but they were made to separate the detainees for one reason or another. Charlie and my friend, Jose Soto, were both on the same floor of the courthouse, but held in separate cells.

"We couldn't see each other, but we could talk to each other," I said while re-counting the experience. "It was like a nightmare. I couldn't believe what was happening. The three of us were there at the court house, but no sign of my cousin Fernando. It doesn't take a genius to know what went down." (49)

While waiting to see the Magistrate Judge for the initial arraignment, I was called into a booth to speak with attorney, Martin I. Isenberg Esq. It was at that time that I was presented with a copy of the criminal complaint.

It had been less than two hours since the arrest that morning, yet by eleven A.M., a detailed complaint logged all the contents in the black duffle bag that was in the back seat of the stolen Buick.

"I wouldn't have had a problem with the complaint except for the fact that it had been submitted to the judge very soon after our arrest. The complaint described a full list of what was in the duffle bag. The problem was that the judge was given the complaint sometime around eleven A.M. that morning, but the discovery reports show that the bag hadn't been inspected until around eight o'clock that night. How did the judge get a full inventory list of the duffle bag at eleven that morning? Unless the police already knew the contents of the bag before hand," I explained.

At eleven-thirty A.M., I, Joseph Rodriguez was in the court room standing before Magistrate Judge Robert B. Kugler for my arraignment. Howard Wiener, Assistant United States Attorney (A.U.S.A.) for Camden's Federal District, represented the government for Camden, New Jersey.

He read the initial charges lodged against me in open court. The A.U.S.A. charged me with possession of firearms, but that was just the beginning.

Although I was indisputably apprehended in possession of a firearm, I pled not guilty, "I knew I had a gun on me, but I really didn't want to be there in the first place. The whole thing stunk. I wasn't pleading guilty to nothing."(50)

Upon my request, the court appointed Martin I Isenberg Esq, a popular pool lawyer in the district, to represent me for the remainder of the case.

In a separate hearing that same morning, Jose Soto also faced Judge Robert B. Kugler. He, too, pled not guilty. Lisa C. Evans was appointed as Jose Soto's Public Defender. Charles Rodriguez, the man the entire fiasco was centered around, followed in our footsteps. With Lisa C. Evans speaking on behalf of Charles, he pled not guilty. Later, attorney Wayne Powell Esq. would be the one to represent my brother, Charles Rodriguez during trial.

Following the hearing that morning, all three of us were transported together in the U.S. Marshall's vehicle to Camden County Prison. There we were officially booked into the custody of the prison, housed in separate units of the jail, and not permitted contact with each other in an attempt to coerce cooperation one against the other.

Several days later, we were transported back to the Camden County Federal Courthouse. On September 4, 1998, Magistrate Judge Robert B. Kugler determined that me, Charles "Crazy Charlie" Rodriguez, and Jose Soto were to be detained pending trial. We were officially declared criminal defendants, and returned to Camden County Prison. Still housed separately, the three of us were unaware of what was happening to each other. After a short stay in Camden, we were again shackled from our hands to our waist, placed together in a van and transported. This time, just Charlie and I were escorted by police vehicles and armed U.S. Marshals, to Fairton, New Jersey where we would be held until their case further developed, on the holdover unit of the medium security prison. Jose Soto was not with us.

On September 15, 1998, an indictment was filed officially charging Jose Soto and the Rodriguez brothers with conspiracy and conspiracy to commit robbery. With no knowledge of what was happening with Jose, me and my brother endured a three week layover, before once again getting relocated. The brothers arrived at Union County Prison in Newark, New Jersey. There they would be officially charged by the Federal Government and held to stand trial in the United States District Court, District of New Jersey.

Still placed in separate housing units at the Union County Jail, the officers allowed us; the Rodriguez brothers to at least re-establish contact with each other. Here, we were permitted to move throughout the jail at designated times and to regulated locations in the prison. Charlie and I first met in the prison library to discuss our case. Unbeknownst to us, Jose Soto, too, was at the Union County Prison. Drawn to the library to research our case, the three of us were finally reunited for the first time in weeks. Finally, together again, Jose told me and Charlie, "They kept me bouncing around from place to place. I couldn't settle there. They offered me ten years to cooperate against you, but because I always said no, they kept moving me around."

CHAPTER 34

On October 5, 1998, the three of us were brought before the Federal District Judge, Honorable Joseph A. Greenway. Once in the courtroom, the three of us were introduced to our Federal Prosecutor for the first time. Assistant United States Attorney (A.U.S.A.), Stuart Rabner, was there to represent the government. Howard Weiner, A.U.S.A. for Camden, was also at the prosecutor's table with Rabner, awaiting his chance to assist the government in any way he could. Weiner had taken such a personal interest in the Rodriguez/Soto case that he followed it all the way to Newark, which was three hours away from Camden County.

During the October 5 hearing, Soto and my brother and I once again pled not guilty to the charges. We listened as A.U.S.A. Rabner explained to the judge the complexity of the particular case and asked for an extension of time in order to further establish ties between the defendants and an ongoing investigation into a string of bank robberies in the Camden area.

Rabner argued that the seventy-two day speedy trial rule would hinder the government's intent to supersede the defendant's original charges, and that the extension of time was necessary.

"In the interest of justice," the judge granted the extension.

As if the situation wasn't bleak enough, on January 15, 1999, the government followed through with their promise of a superseding indictment. The indictment explained that sometime between July 19, 1997 and May 23, 1998, a string of bank robberies spread throughout the Camden area. The superseding indictment charged Soto and the Rodriguez brothers with three of those unsolved robberies.

"That was crazy. How could they name me as a suspect for those robberies? They had me under surveillance since my brother was named a suspect in the shooting of the officer. How could I take part in a bank robbery without getting myself locked-up?" (51) Nonetheless, all three of us were officially charged with the robberies at the Core States Bank on July 19, the Cherry Hill Bank on January 20, 1998; and the Commerce Bank on May 23, 1998.

The government had to bring those bank charges to the Grand Jury five times before they could actually secure the superseding indictment. That's how weak the evidence really was. It wasn't until after the America's T.V. crime segment on my brother's capture and their speculation as to his involvement in several bank robberies that the grand jury finally agreed to indict. It was all a crock. They also said that my brother used a machine gun to shoot Officer Leoni. But we learned all that was a lie." (52)

Although A.U.S.A Rabner wanted to follow through with the prosecution of all three robberies, on March 16, 1999, he was forced to motion to the court for the reciprocal discovery. The government had to revise another indictment, this one omitting the counts involving the Cherry Hill robbery.

According to Joseph Rodriguez, "The prosecution claimed that they really didn't need the Cherry Hill robbery. The truth was the charges couldn't stick. Ten people from that robbery described one or more 'African Americans' that had participated in that robbery. The three of us are all Hispanics with very light skin. The descriptions would not have held up in court, so they dropped that robbery from the indictment. Hell, the witnesses in the other robberies gave different descriptions that didn't quite match us also. The witnesses could only assume that the robbers were Hispanic. They couldn't actually identify anyone. Still, those robberies remained on the indictment."

Although there were obvious discrepancies in witness descriptions, and a lack of physical evidence, all three of us were held for trial on the final indictment.

Initially, Jose, my brother and I were to be charged with provoking the officers into firing their weapons. That part of the case was not pursued. The authorities explained to the public that, "The indictment does not refer to the shootout with police, a decision made by U.S. Attorney's office, to avoid the appearance of potential prejudicial publicity.. .."(53)

In truth, further investigation showed that none of us actually fired any shots, and the circumstances surrounding that shooting became a bit unclear. We explained that we never once gave the authorities a reason to fire upon us.

Yet, throughout the pre-trial investigation, many revelations were brought out into the light. Our own cousin, Fernando Flores' cooperation in the sting operation became fully apparent. As if being setup by one's own family member wasn't enough, the disturbing reality of what the F.B.I.'s true intentions were only compounded the anxiety felt by those who were targeted, "We were setup to be killed. We were never supposed to make it to trial."(54)

Despite the best efforts of the agents involved, we did survive. The F.B.I, was forced to justify their own actions-actions bordering on illegalthat were revealed by the investigation. "There are supposed to be laws protecting people from these kinds of setup operations. Nobody here is claiming to be a saint, but what the F.B.I, did to get us caught up was outside even their own supposed boundaries." (55)

With the F.B.I's entrapment tactics vulnerable to an acquittal by a jury, the government had to be sure that their robbery case against the three defendants was tight enough to secure a conviction. As far as the authorities were concerned, the Rodriguez brothers were public enemy number one, and with Fernando's help, they were almost sure to be successful in keeping them off the streets.

"The whole thing was stupid. They wanted to portray us as some kind of infamous gangsters with no remorse or compassion for anything. That's not entirely true; as our families know. Besides, there wasn't any evidence to put us at the scene of those bank robberies. Nothing! But when you have a puppet willing to be coached, you have all the evidence you need."(56)

And coached he was. I know Fernando didn't know anything about what me and Charlie had been doing with our lives before the F.B.I, approached him. Although Fernando lived in Camden, not far from us, he did not spend much time in our world. Therefore, Fernando could have never had the information he later testified to. In an interview with Lisa C. Evans, Jose E. Soto's Public Defender, Fernando said, "I was told specifics about the vehicles and weapons used and the clothing worn during the robberies."(57) This deposition between Fernando and Lisa C. Evans was held after the trial.

The F.B.I really didn't have any concrete evidence against me, my brother, or Soto, concerning the bank robberies. But they planned ahead. I believe when the F.B.I supplied Fernando with the guns that would be used to facilitate a phony armed robbery; they predetermined what they wanted logged into evidence. Wigs were provided, a red-colored windbreaker and weapons, especially the J-15 assault rifle.

The significance of these items lay in the fact that these items were similar to what was seen in surveillance footage recorded at one of the bank robberies. The wig was found discarded at the scene of the CoreStates bank robbery. The windbreaker was worn by one of the robbery suspects from the same bank.

I, Joseph Rodriguez believe this is very convenient. Those items were provided to me by the F.B.I.'s own informant. Later, the government would use those items in court to make comparisons between what was found on us and what information they had on some of the bank robberies. Still, the windbreaker and the wig did not amount to much. The red windbreaker was as common as any sold in a clothing store or consignment shop. The wigs were more important. Hair samples were found in a wig that had been collected at the scene of one of the bank robberies. Hair was taken from each of us and submitted for analysis. No match was ever made between our hair and the hair inside the wig found at the bank.

The J-15 assault rifle posed a different problem. It is similar to an M-16 assault weapon and would provoke fearful emotions in the hearts of the jurors. The weapon found in possession of the defendants was very similar to the gun shown in a grainy black and white still photo from one of the surveillance cameras from a bank. Although the weapons were similar, it was virtually impossible to positively match the two guns simply by using the inconclusive photo, or the eye witness accounts. In a world obsessed with manufacturing guns, there are dozens of possibilities as to the make and model of the gun used in the bank robbery photo. Gun manufacturers from all over the United States more than a dozen companies apply similar methods of construction, using similar materials.

It was considered, by me, prudent of the government to try to stress to a jury of laymen's, in respect to firearms that the weapons found on us and the weapon used in the bank robberies were the same weapon. The government, on the other hand, knew about the complexities involved in manufacturing guns. They knew it would be difficult for a jury to definitively match the gun from the banks and the gun found with us, the defendants. Still, I believed that the F.B.I, deliberately supplied Fernando Flores with items similar to what was logged as evidence in the bank robbery investigation solely to strengthen their case against me and my brother.

During the trial, eye witness testimony from the victims of the robberies was inconclusive as well. Although Jose Soto, my brother and I are Hispanic males, all three of us were born and raised in Camden, New Jersey. Neither of us spoke Spanish very well; however, several of the bank tellers stated that they heard the robbers speak and described their dialogue as being that of a, "Spanish"(58) or "Mexican"(59) accent. This description is indicative of the suspects having spoken fluent Spanish, which was not the case regarding us.

Not one clear description could be made by any of the bank tellers. The F.B.I, knew this. By supplying Fernando with all the gear and items found in the Buick, they intended to match physical evidence in the car to the physical evidence found at the robbery scenes and from the surveillance footage. I, Joseph Rodriguez believed that it was all very well planned out. Since the F.B.I, intended to kill the suspects anyway, there was supposed to be no trial and no one to dispute the planted evidence. Yet, since we all survived, the F.B.I however, had to use the planted evidence from the duffle bag to sway the jury in their favor. With Fernando's help, they would play off the concerns of everyday citizens, which was a common practice amongst prosecutors. It is my opinion that the F.B.I was so obsessed with securing a conviction against us, especially Charlie that all manner of respect for the law was willfully set aside. Special Agent John Tamm, a non Hispanic, with no knowledge of the language, went so far as to interview a Spanish speaking woman and interpreted her broken English as he saw fit:

"Tamm advised that during the July 19, 1997 robbery of the CoreStates Bank in Woodlyn New Jersey, a female witness was walking her dog near the bank and observed the robbers flee. Subsequently, the agents gained her cooperation and she advised of personally knowing Charles Rodriguez and observed him fleeing the bank and removing his ski mask. This witness advised that Rodriguez had come to her and said he would kill her if she told the police he was involved in the robbery." (60)

It sounds frightening, and Charles Rodriguez should be punished, but was the translation written by S. A. John Tamm the true translation? The same witness was also interviewed by Detective Edwin A. Ramos, a Hispanic male who was fluent in Spanish. Detective Ramos acted as a proper Spanish interpreter. In his report, he said the witness said the following:

"During the morning of July 19, 1997, she was walking her dog on Woodlyn Street...observed four males wearing fatigue clothing and carrying weapons running across a vacant lot. They entered a four-door sedan. She advised one of the males turned to her and stated, "if you say anything, be sure we'll be back to get you'...be advised the statement was made to her in English... Be advised the males were wearing masks, therefore she could not see their faces. She advised one of the males was carrying a rifle and tried to conceal it, by carrying it vertically against his body and under his armpit...she also advised she knows Charles Rodriguez, considering that he grew up in her neighborhood...she could not say if one of the males was Charles Rodriguez, as all of the males were wearing masks...Finally, however she did advised that she may be able to recognize the clothing the individuals were wearing. "(61)

The two translations clearly contradict each other. In S.A. John Tamm's interview, the witness was translated as saying, "Charles Rodriguez removing his mask." But in the interview with Edwin A. Ramos, while S.A. Tamm was also present, the witness made it clear that she, "...could not say if one of the males wearing masks was Charles Rodriguez...."

Was S.A. Tamm's version of the translation an act of malice in order to help sway the case the government's way? Or, due to his lack of understanding for the Spanish language, was it just a genuine misinterpretation? The discrepancies in the two translations were observed and corrected, but for me, the government was playing dirty and not all the underhanded tactics were exposed.

Not one shred of evidence presented at trial sufficiently linked the Rodriguez brothers, or Jose Soto, to any of the bank robberies. The only witness who could put the defendants at the scene of the robberies was Fernando Flores, who was also the government's entire case.

Was Fernando a credible witness?

The Rodriguez brothers think not.

CHAPTER 35
Narrative Summary of the Trial

Thursday, May 20, 1999 was day one of the trial. In his opening statement, Joseph Rodriguez's defense attorney, Martin I Isenberg Esq., addressed the jury, "Innocent until all the evidence is heard. The trial is like a story. It's also like a puzzle. Pieces have to be put together. Joe will take the stand to tell you the armored car robbery was hatched, created, and formulated by the U.S. Government through Fernando Flores. He was paid forty-thousand-eight hundred dollars. All of the money. The banks, no ID., no fingerprints; that will raise reasonable doubt. Yes, these crimes were scary. Don't be blinded by that, however." (Tr.Tr.)

During opening statements, David Holman, co-counsel for Lisa C. Evans, spoke to the jury, on behalf of Jose Soto,

"Yes, Jose was at the rest stop. He got involved in an attempt to rob an armored car. What you're going to learn is why. It was Fernando Flores plan, an inside job, easy money, no problem because his friend worked for the armored car company, and his friend was in trouble with a serious debt, we have to make it look good. All details come from Fernando Flores; the time, the place, the day. All to lure Soto, and to entice him. There were fingerprints, ballistic tests performed, hair fiber tests. Yet, nothing links Soto to these banks. There's a real lack of scientific evidence, credible and reliable evidence with respect to these bank robberies." (Tr. Tr.)

Mr. Wayne Powell, Charles Rodriguez's defense attorney, let it be known that the government's case survived off one major organ, Fernando Flores. In his opening statement that same morning, he said,

"This case will come up short. They need a little fright insurance to feel fear. The F.B.I has the most sophisticated forensic scientific laboratory probably in the world. The government can't produce for you one single shred of credible scientific evidence that any of these three defendants were involved in either of the two bank robberies. Fernando Flores is the government's entire case. You have to believe Fernando Flores, before you put any of the defendants at a bank robbery.

It is clear that Fernando Flores was an essential part of the conviction of the Rodriguez brothers and Jose Soto. With so much placed on the testimony of Fernando, it is fair to question his credibility. During Fernando's testimony at trial, it could certainly be said that he was a little less than truthful in some of his answers. For example, in his May 27, 1999 testimony, Fernando admitted to having a large gun collection. He says, "I kept my guns at my dad's house and my house. I had a gun safe for eight hundred dollars." (62)

Later, after the trial, in a June 21, 2000 interview with Lisa C. Evans, Soto's attorney, Fernando says that he lied on the stand, "… I never had a safe in my apartment." (63) When asked by Lisa C. Evans why he said on the stand that he had a safe for his guns, when he really didn't, he simply replied, "I have no idea."(64)

In one of his statements to the jury, Fernando admitted to lying when it benefited him. When attorney Lisa C. Evans rooted him on cross examination on June 9, 1999, she was able to bring out some of Fernando's true identity, "How is it that you were able to become a police officer, if you did not have a GED certificate or a high school diploma,"(65) she asked him.

Fernando answered, "I don't know." (66)

Lisa C. Evans was not satisfied with that response. She continued to push, "In other words, you lied, is that fair to say."(67)

To the jury, Fernando said, "That's fair to say, yeah," (68) When asked if he felt it was acceptable to stretch the truth, he responded by saying, "Depends on the circumstances."(69)

Perhaps one of the most controversial statements made by Fernando during his testimony is when he told the jury that the government never showed him photos of the bank robberies. On June 8, 1999, Attorney Martin I. Isenberg defense for Joseph Rodriguez, cross examined Fernando concerning his knowledge of the bank robberies. When Isenberg asked, "Did they (F.B.I.) show you photos," (70) Fernando responded, "No."(71)

In a statement later given to Lisa C. Evans, about six months after the trial, Fernando admitted, "I testified in Federal Court as the government's key witness in this case. During trial prep for this case, I was shown surveillance photos from one bank robbery in which I saw three armed men, in the bank lobby, wearing dark clothing. I was also given reports to read about this incident. I was told specifics about the vehicles and weapons used and the clothing worn during these bank robberies. I was told about an incident in which occurred during one of the bank robberies. This had to do with a bank customer who was held up at gun point and car jacked, specifically female. Another incident is where one of the robbers shot up the front door of a bank. In this particular incident, an employee of the bank was walking towards the front doors to open for business and noticed a person wearing dark clothing, holding a weapon. As the employee moved away from the door, this person open fired and entered the bank. This bank was then robbed. "(72)

To the jury, Fernando made the distinction that, "he (Joseph Rodriguez) mentioned that he did a job and the vehicle broke down and they had to car jack another vehicle from the parking lot to get away."(73) Yet in Fernando's statement to Lisa Evans, he clearly tells a different version of how he came by the information concerning the carjacking.

The government's entire case on the bank robberies rested on testimony of an admitted liar. Fernando admitted on the stand to the jury that he had a tendency to lie when the circumstances were right. He even admitted in his later disposition with Lisa C. Evans that he had lied. Unfortunately, the jury was unable to see through Fernando's smoke screen. They were so terrified by the persona of the Rodriguez brothers depicted by the prosecutor and Fernando; therefore they never stood a fair chance.

The prosecution told the jury a story about monsters, and then gave those monsters the faces of Jose Soto and the Rodriguez brothers. Assistant United States Attorneys, Stuart Rabner and Howard Weiner preyed on the concerns of everyday citizens, hoping to sway the trial their own way. In the end, the jury convicted the Rodriguez brothers of all counts of the indictment. Joseph Rodriguez believes the conviction came more out of fear than from the facts of the case.

The facts of this case are simple. Yes, it is true that the men who committed the bank robberies were reckless and very dangerous, but the physical evidence presented during the trial produced no solid links between the defendants and the bank robberies. Forensic evidence proved nothing. The eye witness accounts, though frightening, were entirely inconclusive; and the only person who could place any of the defendants at the scene of the banks was the questionable source, Fernando Flores.

Joseph Rodriguez feels that the trial was well choreographed by the government. The F.B.I. had to be sure that even if the "sting" operation failed under the entrapment defenses, that they still secured a conviction. By bringing the bank robbery charges in with the charges from the Walt Whitman Service Plaza ordeal, they strengthened their odds of a conviction. They coached Fernando by giving him facts of the robberies. They even made it difficult for the defense to find a potential key witness for testimony.

Brenda Bennet lived with Fernando Flores the entire time he was setting up his cousins. Although she was witness to several elements of the setup, she was never given the opportunity to testify in open court about the things she heard and saw. Brenda was privy to inside information that could have potentially devastated the prosecution's case by bringing into question Fernando's credibility. If allowed, Brenda would've testified to the horrendous abuse she suffered at the hands of Fernando. She would've testified to a telephone conversation she overheard Fernando having, where he asked someone about a bulletproof vest.

Most importantly, she would have testified that she personally witnessed Fernando, not Joseph, enter their home with a duffle bag full of firearms. She would've testified that Fernando, in fact, later admitted to her that the F.B.I, supplied him with all the guns the government used to buld their case against us.

Unfortunately, the jury would never get to hear Brenda's side of the story. Before the case would ever see trial, she was forced out of New Jersey to Florida, as a result of constant harassment by the F.B.I, and the incessant threats made by Fernando. Therefore, she would be unavailable to the defense.

CHAPTER 36

For three days the jury deliberated. On July 9, 1999, they returned a verdict of guilty. The verdict was not decided evenly concerning the three defendants. Charles Rodriguez was found guilty on counts, 1, 2, 3, 4, 5, 6, 7, 8 and 9 of the indictment. Joseph Rodriguez was found guilty on counts 1, 2, 3, 4, 5, 6, 7, 8, and 10. Jose Soto was determined to be guilty on counts 1, 7, 8, and 11.

Although Fernando explicitly implicated Soto in the bank robberies with the Rodriguez brothers, he was not found guilty of any of them. The Rodriguez brothers and Soto faced a jury together, yet they were not equally punished. The three defendants were, however, all found guilty of conspiracy for taking part in a phony armored car robbery and for possessing the weapons found in the duffle bag.

The sentencing in this case could be considered very steep to some, but others may feel justice was served. For Charlie, on count 1 of the indictment, the court handed down a 60 month sentence; counts 2 and 4, 175 months to run concurrently (74) with one another and with count 1; for count 3, 60 months to run consecutive (75) to all counts; count 5, 240 months to run consecutive to all counts; for count 6, 175 months to run concurrently with counts 1,2, and 4; count 7, 175 months to run concurrently with counts 1,2,4 and 6; count 8, a term of life imprisonment to run consecutively with counts; and count 9, 120 months to run concurrently with all counts 1,2,4, 6, and 7.

The overall sentence for Charles Rodriguez equaled to life imprisonment with 475 months (39 years) to run consecutively.

Joseph Rodriguez suffered a similar fate. For count 1, he too received 60 months; for counts 2 and 4, 135 months concurrent with one another and with count 1. For count 3, 60 months to run consecutive to all counts; count 5, 240 months to run consecutive to all counts; count 6, 135 months to run concurrently with counts 1, 2 and 4, count 7, 135 months to run concurrently with counts 1, 2, 4; and 6; for count 8, he received a term of life imprisonment to run consecutive with all counts; and for count 10, 120 months to run concurrently with counts 1,2,4, 6 and 7.

Joseph Rodriguez received life imprisonment, plus an additional 435 months (35 years).

As for Jose Soto, he received 60 months on count 1; count 7, 87 months to run concurrently with count 1; count 8, 360 months to run consecutive to all counts; count 11, 87 months to run concurrently with counts 1 and 7.

Jose received a total of 447 months, over 37 years.

The Rodriguez brothers received a life sentence, plus many years included with the life. Jose Soto received 37 years, which is considered a de facto life sentence, or in layman's terms, "might as well be a life sentence." So many years handed down by the court, due to the sentencing schemes required by the guidelines that were in place at the time of sentencing, yet no one ever died in this case.

Also troubling issue is the fact that the robbery charges rested on the testimony of a man whose credibility has severely come into question. Fernando Flores took the stand and testified at hearings, but changed his story each time. During the trial, he testified on behalf of the government and implicated all three defendants in criminal acts.

Several months later, on June 21, 2000, Fernando recanted his testimony in an interview with Lisa C. Evans, defense attorney for Jose Soto. Again, several years later, on July 10, 2003, Fernando changed his position during a Rule 33 hearing. This was a hearing that basically argued for a new trial. The hearing was presided over by the original trial judge, The Honorable Joseph A. Greenway.

Did Fernando really tell the truth, or did he lie to receive benefits from the government? One must build their own opinion. To follow are two recorded testimonies by Fernando Flores.

UNITED STATES DISTRICT COURT
DISTRICT OF NEW JERSEY

UNITED STATES OF AMERICA,　　　　. Case No.98-5470-003

　　　　　　Plaintiff,　　　　. 800 Hudson Square
　　-vs-　　　　　　　　　　. Suite 350
　　　　　　　　　　　　. Camden, New Jersey 08101
JOSE SOTO,

　　　　　　Defendant,
　　　　　　　　　　　　.　　June 21, 2000

TRANSCRIPT OF INTERVIEW
BETWEEN
LISA C. EVANS AND FERNANDO FLORES

Transcript recorded by electronic sound recording, transcript
produced by transcription service.

J&J COURT TRANSCRIBERS, INC.
268 Evergreen Avenue Hamilton,
New Jersey 08619
(609) 586-2311　Fax No. (609) 587-3599

1   MS. EVANS: Today is June 21st, 2000. This is Lisa
2   C. Evans, Assistant Federal Public Defender. I'm here in my
3   office at 800 Hudson Square, Suite 350, Camden, New Jersey,
4   with my investigator, Maureen Lee, and with Fernando Flores.
5   Mr. Flores has contacted this office and indicated he
6   wished to come in to give a statement regarding the case of
7   United States versus Jose Soto, 98-547-003, Judge Joseph A.
8   Greenaway. When Mr. Flores came in about 25 minutes ago, I had
9   him sign an affidavit. Mr. Flores, would you state your name,
10 please?
11   MR. FLORES: Fernando Flores.
12   MS. EVANS: And, your date of birth? Can you speak
13 up?
14   MR. FLORES: 12/9/72.
15   MS. EVANS: And, are you here, today, to give a
16 statement regarding the matter of United States versus Jose
17 Soto?
18   MR. FLORES: Yes.
19   MS. EVANS: Are you here under your own free will?
20   MR. FLORES: Yes.
21   MS. EVANS: Has anyone forced, coerced, or threatened
22 you to come in and give a statement today?
23   MR. FLORES: No.
24   MS. EVANS: And, has anyone promised you, or given
25 you any compensation, or promised you anything, in exchange for

```
 1    coming in to give this statement?
 2              MR. FLORES:  No.
 3              MS. EVANS:  And/ did you sign an affidavit today,
 4         attesting to those questions that I just asked you?
 5              MR. FLORES:  Yes.
 6              MS. EVANS:  Okay.  Now — and, you're giving this
 7    statement today, why?
 8              MR. FLORES:  Because I feel as though I have some
 9    information that could be — that's important to the case.
10              MS. EVANS:  Okay.  You have some information that's
11    important to the case.  Now, the information that you have that
12    you think is important to the case that we should know about,
13    what is that information?  What is that information regarding?
14              MR. FLORES:  It's regarding the incident on September
15    1st.
16              MS. EVANS:  The incident September 1st.  And, what is
17    it about that incident on September 1st that you think we should
18    be aware of?
19              MR. FLORES:  Just that a —
20              MS. EVANS:  And, we should say September 1st, 1998?
21              MR. FLORES:  Yes.
22              MS. EVANS:  The rest stop?
23              MR. FLORES:  Yes.
24              MS. EVANS:  Incident involving my client, Jose Soto,
25    Charles Rodriguez, and Joseph Rodriguez.  Is that correct?
```

J&J COURT TRANSCRIBERS, INC.

196

```
 1              MR. FLORES: Yes. Yes.

 2              MS. EVANS: Okay. What information do you think we

 3     should be aware of?

 4              MR. FLORES: Just information — comments that I've

 5     heard —

 6              MS. EVANS: Urn-hum?

 7              MR. FLORES: — about the incident.

 8              MS. EVANS: Okay. Anything else? Well, let me ask

 9     you this, what kind of comments did you hear, and from who?

10              MR. FLORES: One of the comments I heard was that

11     "the deader the better."

12              MS. EVANS: "The deader the better"? Okay. Deader

13     -- d-e-a-d-e-r? What, exactly, do you mean by that?

14              MR. FLORES: That they wanted these guys dead.

15              MS. EVANS: Okay. Now, who is 'they"?

16              MR. FLORES: The FBI.

17              MS. EVANS: The FBI? And, who is "these guys"?

18              MR. FLORES: 'These guys" are Jose Soto, Charles

19     Rodriguez and Joseph Rodriguez.

20              MS. EVANS: Okay. And, when you say 'the .FBI," can

21     you be more specific? Are there particular agents that you're

22     referring to?

23              MR. FLORES: The one agent that made a comment at 24 that

24     time was Agent John Tan (phonetic).

25              MS. EVANS: Okay. And, when did John Tan make this
```

```
 1  comment?                                                      5

 2          MR. FLORES:  The comment was made prior to September

 3  1st.

 4          MS. EVANS:  Prior to September 1st.  Do you remember

 5  the date?

 6          MR. FLORES:  No, I don't.

 7          MS. EVANS:  Do you remember the — you met with Tan

 8  on several occasions?

 9          MR. FLORES:  Yes.

10          MS. EVANS:  Prior to September 1st.  Is that correct?

11          MR. FLORES:  Yes.

12          MS. EVANS:  Do you remember if it was said during the

13  first meeting?

14          MR. FLORES:  No.

15          MS. EVANS:  During the second meeting?

16          MR. FLORES:  No.  It was probably said about a week

17  before the incident.

18          MS. EVANS:  About a week before the incident?

19          MR. FLORES:  Yes.

20          MS. EVANS:  And, where were you when Agent Tan made

21  this statement?

22          MR. FLORES:  I believe we met — at a location, but I

23  don't remember where.

24          MS. EVANS:  You don't remember where?  Was it in his

25  office?


                    J&J COURT TRANSCRIBERS, INC.
```

1   MR. FLORES: No.

2   MS. EVANS: Okay. Was it at your home?

3   MR. FLORES: No. It was on the road, I believe.

4   MS. EVANS: It was on the road? And, was anyone else

5   present when Agent John Tan made this statement to you?

6   MR. FLORES: No.

7   MS. EVANS: And, what was the context of the

8   statement, 'The deader the better"? What were you talking

9   about when that statement was made?

10   MR. FLORES: We were talking about the — setting up,

11   I guess, the armored car robbery, and the question I had was,

12   why don't we take these guys down in my apartment, or, we'll

13   stop these guys on the way to my apartment. I mean, he just

14   kept going — the officer said, no, we want them at the rest

15   stop, and, I believe, not too much after that, that's when the

16   comment was made, "The deader the better."

17   MS. EVANS: Okay. And, what — did he say anything

18   else after that, or before that, that would support that

19   comment?

20   MR. FLORES: Not very much. No.

21   MS. EVANS: And, what was your perception of that

22   comment? What did you believe he meant by that, and by the

23   conversation before and after the comment?

24   MR. FLORES: My belief was that they did not want to

25   take these guys alive, because, if they wanted to, they could

1 have took them down on several occasions prior to the rest

2 stop. And, by him saying -- by him making that comment, it was

3 my understanding that he wanted these guys dead.

4   MS. EVANS: Now, you said that they could have taken

5 them down several times prior to the rest stop. What times would

6 they have had an opportunity to take them down?

7   MR. FLORES: On their way to my apartment, early in the

8 morning. They knew that the weapons were in my apartment,

9 and that the only possible weapon would have been what Charlie

10 was carrying. They could have took them down in my apartment,

11 because it wasn't until about an hour and a half, maybe two

12 hours after they were there that they started loading the

13 weapons up.

14   MS. EVANS: Okay. So, weapons were your -- in your

15 apartment were not loaded?

16   MR. FLORES: Were not loaded. No.

17   MS. EVANS: Okay.

18   MR. FLORES: The magazines were, but the weapons were

19 Not.

20   MS. EVANS: All right. So, the magazines were not in

21 the weapon?

22   MR. FLORES: Not at the time. No.

23   MS. EVANS: And, was that something that was pre-

24 arranged by the FBI, that the magazines would not be loaded?

25   MR. FLORES: No, that's just the way it happened.

```
 1   MS. EVANS:  Just the way it happened?  Were they -
 2   do you know if they were aware of that fact?
 3              MR. FLORES:  Who?
 4              MS. EVANS:  The FBI.
 5              MR. 'FLORES:  Yes, because there were - one of the
 6   requests that Joe had was, Joe said, don't mess with these
 7   guns.  Don't play with them.  And, I have little kids at home, so
 8   I don't want to keep no loaded weapons, you know, somewhere
 9   were the kids can just reach in the bag, and grab -- I didn't want
10   that, either.
11              MS. EVANS:  And, what time did Joe arrive, or Joe,
12   Jose and Charlie arrive to your house that morning?
13              MR. FLORES:  I would say approximately five, five
14   a.m.
15              MS. EVANS MS. EVANS:  And, at that time, were the weapons
16   loaded?
17              MR. FLORES:  No, they were not.
18              MS. EVANS:  Okay.  And, when did you start loading
19   the weapons?
20              MR. FLORES:  We started loading the weapons, I would say,
21   approximately eight o'clock.
22              MS. EVANS:  Eight o'clock.  So, they were in your
23   apartment several hours prior to the weapons being loaded?
24              MR. FLORES:  Yes.
25              MS. EVANS:  Now, was there any communication by you
```

1 to the FBI during that time, after five, but before eight,
2 before the weapons were loaded?
3   MR. FLORES: Yeah. I believe, before seven — before
4 the guys started loading up the weapons, and the time they got
5 There - - I did leave my apartment, when I went to the 7-Eleven
6 to go buy some orange juice and film, because I forget —
7   MS. EVANS: Urn-hum. And, at that time, did you have
8 communication with the FBI?
9   MR. FLORES: Yes, I did.
10   MS. EVANS: And, you testified to that at trial? Is
11 that correct?
12   MR. FLORES: Yes.
13   MS. EVANS: Okay. Now, you — gave, at trial, some
14 explanation as to why the defendants were not arrested at your
15 apartment. Do you recall what explanation you gave?
16   MR. FLORES: The explanation I gave that they told me
17 was that the — they didn't want to risk a Shootout in a
18 residential neighborhood.
19   MS. EVANS: That's what the -- who told you?
20   MR. FLORES: The FBI told me.
21   MS. EVANS: And, when did they tell you that?
22   MR FLORES: This was discussed, I guess, during the
23 planning of the armored car robbery.
24   MS. EVANS: During the planning of the armored car
25 robbery. During your — was it discussed in preparation for

1 trial?

2   MR. FLORES: Yes.

3   MS. EVANS: And, what did they tell you in
4 preparation for trial?

5   MR. FLORES: What they said 'was that the reason that
6 they didn't want to take them down at the apartment was they
7 didn't want to risk a shoo tout in a residential neighborhood.

8   MS. EVANS: Okay. What was your response to that?

9   MR. FLORES: Well, I don't think I had any, any say
10 in that.

11   MS. EVANS: Did you say something to them? Or, what
12 provoked that conversation?

13   MR. FLORES: Well — I think I brought up in
14 conversation -- why don't you just take these guys down in my
15 apartment.? You know, there's no guns. They had no — the guns
16 were in the bag. The guns weren't loaded. If there was a gun
17 loaded, it was the one that Charlie had on him. I said, you
18 know, bring all the guys you want. And, just storm the
19 apartment. You could take these guys down.

20   MS. EVANS: Urn-hum.

21   MR. FLORES: I said, you have a greater risk at a
22 rest stop, because you know these guys are going to be loaded
23 for bear.

24   MS. EVANS: Right. And, what was the response when
25 you said that?

1   MR. FLORES: I believe they said they'll be ready.

2   MS. EVANS: Okay.

3   MR. FLORES: They said, just go with the plan. I
4 don't see why they would rather face these guys fully loaded
5 than just face one guy with a gun. I don't know why. But,
6 that's the way they wanted to do it.

7   MS. EVANS: Now, when -- after the - let me ask you
8 this. During the rest stop incident, was there ever a time
9 where you heard gun shots from inside the car?

10   MR. FLORES: No.

11   MS. EVANS: And, was there discussion regarding that

12 after the rest stop incident?

13   MR. FLORES: After the rest stop incident, yeah.
14 It was--well, I guess, my first interview, they said, well, did
15 you hear a loud - did you hear a loud bang first, and then
16 multiple shots afterward? Or, what did you hear? I got the
17 impression that they wanted me to say, yeah, that I heard a
18 loud shot, first, then I heard multiple shots afterwards.

19   MS. EVANS: Um-hum.

20   MR. FLORES: And, I believe they said that - well,
21 after the incident, before the trial, they said that somebody
22 out of the car shot a gun.

23   MS. EVANS: Urn-hum.

24   MR. FLORES: And, I later found out that it' s not
25 true.

J&J COURT TRANSCRIBERS, INC.

1   MS. EVANS: Did you testify that you heard a loud

2   shot coming out of the car?

3   MR. FLORES: Yes.

4   MS. EVANS: Did you testify to that because it was

5   true? Or, because of some other reason?

6   MR. FLORES: I testified to that because that's what

7   they told me what happened.

8   MS. EVANS: Okay. That's what they told you what

9   happened?

10   MR. FLORES: They told me that's what happened. Yes.

11   MS. EVANS: That's what happened, and so, then you

12   testified — or, you gave a statement, a taped statement?

13   MR. FLORES: Uh-huh.

14   MS. EVANS: On the date — on September 1st,

15   consistent with that?

16   MR. FLORES: Consistent with it. Yes.

17   MS. EVANS: Okay. Did the FBI tell you to say that? Did

18   they say, well, we want you to say this? Or, they — I

19   mean, how did that whole thing go down?

20   MR. FLORES: They didn't tell me — they didn't come

21   try to tell me well, this is what you have to say.

22   Ms. EVANS: Um-hum.

23   MR. FLORES: But, they mentioned that before I made

24   the taped statement.

25   MS. EVANS: Okay. And, you took that as meaning

                J&J COURT TRANSCRIBERS, INC.

1 that's what you should testify, consistent –

2   MR. FLORES: I took that as – yes. That's what I
3 should say in the taped statement.

4   MS. EVANS: Was there any other testimony that you
5 gave at trial that was either not true, or was –- that you were
6 asked to state by the FBI?

7   MR. FLORES: Well, the only other comment I could
8 think of was about Bustano (phonetic).

9   MS. EVANS: Okay.

10   MR. FLORES: And, the question I was – Wayne Powell, I
11 guess, the attorney for Charles Rodriguez, gave me a scanner,
12 told me to turn it on, play with the buttons, look at it, and
13 tell me, do I see a light on the scanner? And, I testified in
14 Court that no, I did not see a light – a red light on the
15 scanner.

16   MS. EVANS: Um-hum.

17   MR. FLORES: So, I believe I testified in Court that I
18 knew that that scanner was on because I noticed a red light
19 indicating that it was on.

20   MS. EVANS: Urn-hum. Now, was that testimony – when
21 you said that – was that testimony true? That you knew it was on
22 because you saw the red light?

23   MR. FLORES: No. I testified that, yeah, I saw the – I
24 testified that I saw the red light, and I knew it was on; but no,
25 I did not see a red light.

J&J COURT **TRANSCRIBERS, INC.**

14

          MS. EVANS: You — right. And, why did you lie about

2 that?

3   MR. FLORES: Because, during trial preparations, they

4 said, well, how did you know the — I was told, well, how did

5 you know the -scanner was on? Was one of the questions. I

6 said, because it had a red light. And — you know, they led me

7 to believe — or, they told me -- the way they — it was

8 discussed, that particular question was, they wanted me to say,

9 yeah, well, you knew it was on because it had a red light.

10   MS. EVANS: Okay.

11   MR. FLORES: But, no, I did not see a red light on

12 the scanner.

13   MS. EVANS: So, you testified to that at trial,

14 because the FBI told you to say that?

15   MR. FLORES: Yes.

16   MS. EVANS: What agent, specifically? Do you recall?

17   MR. FLORES: I don't believe it's an Agent. I

18 believe it was Howard Weiner.

19   MS. EVANS: Howard Weiner. The U.S. Attorney?

20   MR. FLORES: Yes.

21   MS. EVANS: And, when you had that discussion with

22 him, was he aware that you really didn't see a red light?

23   MR. FLORES: Yes.

24   MS. EVANS: Okay. And, how do you know that?

25   MR. FLORES: Because I didn't even see a red light.

J&J COURT TRANSCRIBERS, INC.

1   MS. EVANS: You didn't see a red light? And, you
2 told him that?

3   MR. FLORES: I told him that.

4   MS. EVANS: Okay. Now, so, you come up with the
5 or the testimony that — you had testified to a red
6 light Then, what happened at trial? You testified that there
7 was a red light?

8   MR. FLORES: At trial, I testified there was a red
9 light. I was given the scanner — I was the scanner radio
10 Wayne Powell. looked at the scanner.

11   MS. EVANS: And, that was the cross examination?

12   MR. FLORES: That was on cross examination.

13   MS. EVANS: Okay.

14   MR. FLORES: I didn't see no red light, at all, on,
15 the scanner

16   MS. EVANS: Um-hum.

17   MR. FLORES: The next day, I get back on the stand
18 I'm given the same scanner, and there's a red light on the
19 scanner

20   MS. EVANS: Now, what happened in between? Did
21 something happen in between Mr. Powell cross examining you, and
22 there being no red light, and then Mr. Weiner redirecting you,
23 and there being a red light?

24   Yes. Later on, you know — after the
25 , a phone call was made to another agent, and I believe it

J&J COURT TRANSCRIBERS, INC.

1 was discussed that the — there was supposed to be a red light
2 on the scanner. Or, put a red light on the scanner. The next
3 day, I go to Court, turn the scanner on. I was told to look at
4 it a specific way, and there was a red light on the scanner.
5 An orange light --

6   MS. EVANS: Now, when you say a phone call was made
7 -- what office was this phone call made from?

8   MR. FLORES: The phone call was made from the U.S.
9 Attorney's office.

10   MS. EVANS: And, who was present when the phone call
11 was made?

12   MR. FLORES: Myself, Jim Walsh, Howard Weiner, Stu
13 Mavern (sic). There might have been someone else, but I don't
14 remember.

15   MS. EVANS: And, do you know where the call was made
16 to?

17   MR. FLORES: I have no idea.

18   MS. EVANS: And, do you — who, specifically, made
19 the phone call?

20   MR. FLORES: I believe it was Jim Walsh.

21   MS. EVANS: And, what do you recall Agent Walsh
22 stating during that conversation?

23   MR. FLORES: Just called to, you know, just to look
24 it over. Just told the guy, you have a scanner, and he needed
25 the scanner, or something to that effect.

                    J&J COURT TRANSCRIBERS, INC.

1   MS. EVANS: He needed a red light on the scanner?

2   MR. FLORES: Or, wanted a red light on the scanner.

3   MS. EVANS: Or, wanted a red light on the scanner.

4   MR. FLORES: Yes.

5   MS. EVANS: And, what happened after that?

6   MR. FLORES: After that, we went back to the hotel.

7 Woke up the next day, we got ready to go back to trial, and I

8 was given the same scanner, and it had an orange light on it.

9   MS. EVANS: And, prior to that day, when you — and,

10 that was on redirect by Mr. Weiner, is that correct?

11   MR. FLORES: Yes.

12   MS. EVANS: Prior to that day, had you ever seen a

13 red, or orange light, on that scanner?

14   MR. FLORES: No.

15   MS. EVANS: Either in Court, when you were cross

16 examined by Mr. Powell, or — you can say yes or no to that.

17   MR. FLORES: No, I have to say no to it.

18   MS. EVANS: And, to the apartment? On that same

19 scanner, did you see a red light?

20   MR. FLORES: — the first time 1 saw the scanner, I

21 did not see a red light.

22   MS. EVANS: Was there an orange LCD display on that

23 scanner, at the apartment, or in Court?

24   MR. FLORES: No. The only time I saw the orange

25 light was the day — the second day I was shown the scanner. I

1 guess, it was redirect, I guess, whatever it is, by Howard
2 Weiner.

3   MS. EVANS: Are you aware of any actions taken by the
4 FBI to change the scanner, or to, you know, change the light in
5 the scanner?

6   MR. FLORES: The only thing I can say is that a phone
7 call was made. The next day, I come to Court, and there's an
8 orange light on the scanner.

9   MS. EVANS: Now, there was testimony at trial
10 regarding your -- the guns you had at your home? Is that
11 correct?

12   MR. FLORES: Yes.

13   MS. EVANS: And, there was testimony regarding your
14 guns being maintained, or stored in a safe?

15   MR. FLORES: Yes.

16   MS. EVANS: What can you tell us about that
17 testimony.

18   MR. FLORES: All the guns were not stored in my
19 apartment. That guns were stored in other places.

20   MS. EVANS: Urn-hum.

21   MR. FLORES: And, I never had a safe in my apartment.

22   MS. EVANS: You never had a safe in your apartment?
23 Why did you say you had a safe in your apartment?

24   MR. FLORES: I have no idea why.

25   MS. EVANS: You don't remember? You don't have any

1 idea why you said that? Okay. So, that's not something that
2 was told to you by someone to say?

3   MR. FLORES: No. No.

4   MS. EVANS: And, was there any other testimony — -any
5 testimony regarding what Charlie was going to do, that was
6 given to you by the FBI? Or, a statement?

7   MR. FLORES: The comment that the FBI told me that
8 they heard from Charlie, was that Charlie vowed to not be taken
9 alive. That if he were ever captured, he would not be taken
10 alive.

11   MS. EVANS: Okay. Was there anything else, other
12 than that?

13   MR. FLORES: And, from my understanding, through the
14 family, is that the only reason that he did turn himself in was
15 because — they didn't have enough money for a private
16 attorney.

17   MS. EVANS: Urn-hum?

18   MR. FLORES: And, prior to September 1st, they raided
19 the - house. They thought Charlie was there. And, they put
20 the kid in the hospital that they believed was Charles
21 Rodriguez. They just beat this kid, and broke his leg, and
22 just tore him up. And, that was a lawsuit that happened
23 against the Camden police, and Walsh was there. They thought
24 this kid was Charlie. They banged this kid up bad, put him in
25 the hospital. And, when Charlie heard that, he said, well, you

J&J COURT TRANSCRIBERS, INC.

1 know, I'm not going to turn myself in, if these guys are going
2 to do this to me. You know.

3   MS. EVANS: Right.

4   MR. FLORES: He said, — just trying to, you know,
5 get the family to — him some money, so he could get a private
6 lawyer, so he could turn himself in.

7   MS. EVANS: Do you remember when that incident
8 occurred?

9   MR. FLORES: I believe — it happened in the summer.
10 I believe it happened on Stevens Street.

11   MS. EVANS: Stevens Street?

12   MR. FLORES: Yes.

13   MS. EVANS: Do you remember the name of the person —

14   MR. FLORES: No.

15   MS. EVANS: — who was the victim in that case? Or,
16 the house?

17   MR. FLORES: No. It was the 500 block of Stevens
18 Street, I believe.

19   MS. EVANS: And, do you know whether or not there is
20 any civil litigation pending?

21   MR. FLORES: Yes, the guy that sued whoever was there
22 --Walsh, was there -- broke his leg, they banged him up pretty
23 bad, put him in the hospital.

24   MS. EVANS: They broke his leg?

25   MR. FLORES: Yes. Because they thought he was

                    J&J COURT TRANSCRIBERS, INC.

1 Charlie. And, that's one of the reasons that Charlie didn't
2 want to turn himself in.

3   MS. EVANS: Now, was that incident discussed with any
4 of the agents in this particular case?

5   MR. FLORES: No.

6   MS. EVANS: Or, any of the U.S. Attorneys in this
7 particular case?

8   MR. FLORES: No.

9   MS. EVANS: Is there anything else that you want to
10 inform us about, pertaining to this matter?

11   MR. FLORES: Not at this time.

12   MS. EVANS: Was the information that you provided
13 this afternoon true? Was the information that you provided
14 true and correct?

15   MR. FLORES: Yes.

16   MS. EVANS: There's just one other question that I
17 have for you, if you wouldn't mind. During the testimony at
18 trial, you were questioned by myself regarding Agent John Tan's
19 302's, which is his FBI reports?

20   MR. FLORES: Yes.

21   MS. EVANS: Prior to the trial,- did you see Agent
22 Tan's 302's?

23   MR. FLORES: I was told what was — I was told, on
24 several occasions, what was in them. And understood that what
25 I was testifying to, what I was preparing for trial for, was

1 different from what was on the reports.

2   MS. EVANS: Was different?

3   MR. FLORES: Yes.

4   MS. EVANS: Okay. But, you never saw those reports

5   MR. FLORES: I might have read a paragraph or two

6 from one of them, or a few of them. But, you know, none that I

7 could really —

8   MS. EVANS: And, who told you that it was different?

9   MR. FLORES: Howard Weiner.

10   MS. EVANS: And, in -- do you remember the context of

11 those conversations? Or, what exactly you talked about?

12   MR. FLORES: No, I don't.

13   MS. EVANS: And — okay. So, he said they were

14 different?

15   MR. FLORES: Um-hum. Yes.

16   MS. EVANS: Did you testify consistent to those

17 reports?

18   MR. FLORES: I don't believe I did. No.

19   MS. EVANS: Or, did you testify consistent to what

20 happened?

21   MR. FLORES: I testified to what I believe — what I

22 remember, you know, what happened. But, some information that

23 I testified to was given to me by the FBI.

24   MS. EVANS: Was given to you by the FBI

25   MR. FLORES: Yes.

1   MS. EVANS: Like what?

2   MR. FLORES: I suppose, comments that were made.

3   MS. EVANS: What kind of comments?

4   MS. FLORES: As far as them saying that − − that

5   Charlie said he would not be taken alive.

6   MS. EVANS: Um-hum.

7   MR. FLORES: That the takedown of these guys would

8   have been better suited at the truck rest stop, rather than the

9   residential neighborhood. I don't believe that that was true.

10   MS. EVANS: Um-hum.

11   MR. FLORES: That's what they wanted me to say. And,

12   there was a couple - a couple other comments that I can't

13   MS. EVANS: You can't remember?

14   MR. FLORES: Can't remember right now.

15   MS. EVANS: At this time? Anything Else?

16   MR. FLORES: No.

17   MS. And, again, all that information − all

18   all the information you provided today is true? Is that correct?

19   MS. FLORES: Yes.

20   MS EVANS: No one forced you, or threatened you, or

21   coerced you to provide this information?

22   MR. FLORES: No

23   MS. EVANS: No one has paid you, or promised you any

24   compensation, or anything in exchange for this statement, is

25   that true?

1   MR. FLORES: That is true.

2   MS. EVANS: Okay. Thank you, Mr. Flores

3   * * * * *

4   C E R T I F I C A T I O N

5   I, Tammy DeRisi, certify that the foregoing is a

6 correct transcript from the electronic sound recording of the

7 proceedings in the above-entitled matter.

8

9 _Tammy DeRisi_   Date: 11/14/00

10 Tammy DeRisi

11 J&J COURT TRANSCRIBERS, INC.

12

13

14

15

16

17

18

19

20

21

22

23

24

25

                    J&J COURT TRANSCRIBERS, INC.

I, FERNANDO FLORES TYPED UP A STATEMENT
IN REFERENCE TO AN INCIDENT ON SEPT 1, 1998
THIS STATEMENT IS ON A BLACK DISK. THIS
DISK WAS GIVEN TO DENISE RODRIGUEZ FOR
SAFE KEEPING —
THE STATEMENT ON THIS DISK IS WHAT I
COULD REMEMBER ABOUT THIS INCIDENT NOT
ALL IS INCLUDED.

7.23.00

Fernando Flores

I, FERNANDO FLORES, AM GIVING THIS STATEMENT
ON MY OWN FREE WILL WITHOUT ANY THREATS OR
PROMISES MADE. THIS STATEMENT IS IN REGARDS TO
AN INCIDENT IN WHICH OCCURRED ON SEPT. 1ST,
1998.

I TESTIFIED IN FEDERAL COURT AS THE GOVERN-
MENT'S KEY WITNESS IN THIS CASE. DURING THE
TRIAL PREP FOR THIS CASE, I WAS SHOWN SURVEIL-
LANCE PHOTOS FROM ONE BANK IN WHICH SHOWED
THREE ARMED MEN WEARING DARK CLOTHING IN
THE BANK LOBBY. I WAS ALSO GIVEN FBI REPORTS
TO READ ABOUT THIS INCIDENT. I WAS TOLD SPE-
CIFICS ABOUT THE VEHICLES AND WEAPONS USED,

AND THE CLOTHING WORN DURING THESE BANK ROBBERIES. I WAS ALSO TOLD ABOUT AN INCIDENT IN WHICH OCCURRED DURING ONE OF THE BANK ROBBERIES. THIS HAD TO DO WITH A BANK CUSTOMER OR EMPLOYEE WHO WAS HELD AT GUNPOINT AND CARJACKED (specifically a female). ANOTHER INCIDENT IS WHERE ONE OF THE ROBBERS SHOT UP THE FRONT DOOR OF A BANK. IN THIS PARTICULAR INCIDENT, AN EMPLOYEE OF THE BANK WAS WALKING TOWARDS THE FRONT DOOR TO OPEN FOR BUSINESS AND NOTICED A PERSON WEARING DARK CLOTHING, HOLDING A WEAPON. AS THE EMPLOYEE MOVED AWAY FROM THE DOOR, THIS PERSON OPENED FIRE AND ENTERED THE BANK. THIS BANK WAS THEN ROBBED.

MY INITIAL INVOLVEMENT WAS TO MEET WITH A FEDERAL AGENT WHO ASKED ME IF I WOULD HELP THE FBI IN CAPTURING CHARLES RODRIGUEZ. AT THIS TIME CHARLES WAS WANTED FOR QUESTIONING IN REGARDS TO AN INCIDENT WHERE A POLICE OFFICER WAS SHOT AND INJURED WHILE RESPONDING TO GUNSHOTS IN THE AREA. I WAS ALSO TOLD THAT CHARLES WAS WANTED FOR BANK ROBBERIES. AT FIRST, I WANTED NO PART OF THIS INVESTIGATION AND TOLD THE FEDERAL AGENT THAT I WOULD THINK ABOUT IT. A SECOND MEETING WAS SET AND AT THIS TIME, I WAS TOLD THAT CHARLES HAD THREATENED THE LIFE OF A POLICE OFFICER. I THOUGHT ABOUT IT AND AGREED TO ASSIST IN HIS CAPTURE. I WAS TOLD TO BEFRIEND JOSEPH RODRIGUEZ AND ASKED HIM ABOUT CHARLES WHEREABOUTS. I WAS ALSO TOLD TO OFFER WEAPONS, AMMUNITION AND WHATEVER WAS

NECESSARY IN ORDER TO OBTAIN INFORMATION ON CHARLES WHEREABOUTS. AT THIS MEETING, I RECEIVED INFORMATION THAT CHARLES

AREA. THIS INFORMATION WAS

WAS OK AND IN THE RELAYED TO THE FBI.

DURING A SHORT PERIOD OF TIME, SEVERAL MEETINGS WERE CONDUCTED BETWEEN MYSELF AND JOSEPH, AND MYSELF AND THE FBI TO RELAY WHAT EVER INFORMATION WAS LEARNED. DURING THESE MEETINGS, A DISCUSSION WAS CONDUCTED IN WHICH A PLACE WOULD BE ROBBED (SPECIFICALLY A CHECK CASHING PLACE). AFTER FURTHER DISCUS-SION THIS PLAN WAS DROPPED.

I WAS THEN TOLD TO OFFER JOSEPH PART IN A ROBBERY OF AN ARMORED CAR. AT THIS TIME THE ONLY INFORMATION ABOUT THIS ROBBERY THAT I WAS TOLD TO RELAY TO JOSEPH, WAS THAT A FRIEND OF MINE WHO WORKS FOR THIS PARTICU-LAR COMPANY WAS IN HEAVY GAMBLING DEBT AND WANTED TO GET ROBBED. HE WOULD BE THE INSIDE GUY AND ASSIST IN THE ROBBERY. THE ONLY SPECIF-ICS GIVEN WAS THAT THIS ROBBERY WOULD

OF DOLLARS. MILLIONS

ROBBERY, INVOLVED AND JOSEPH RODRIGUEZ, AND JOSE SOTO, ALONG WITH MY INSIDE GUY. THE PLAN DISCUSSED BETWEEN MYSELF AND THE FBI WAS THAT NO SHOTS WERE TO BE FIRED, BECAUSE I WAS TO DRIVE THE VEHICLE USED IN THIS ROBBERY. THE SPECIFICS ABOUT THIS ROBBERY WAS THAT MY INSIDE GUY WOULD BE RIDING IN AN ARMORED CAR THAT WOULD BE MAKING A DROP AT A NEW JERSEY TURNPIKE REST STOP. AS HE EXITS THE TRUCK, I WOULD DRIVE UP AND MY GUYS WOULD

ROB HIM. HE WAS TO HAND OVER THE MONEY, AND WE WOULD DRIVE OFF WITH NO SHOTS FIRED OR ANYONE GETTING HURT. AT THE TURNPIKE REST STOP THE VEHICLE I WAS DRIVING WAS RAMMED SEVERAL TIMES BY A TOW TRUCK AND SHOT NUMEROUS TIMES BY POLICE GUNFIRE. EVERYONE WAS ARRESTED AND TRANSPORTED ACCORDINGLY. I LATER TESTIFIED IN COURT AFTER BEING ASSURED THAT ME AND MY FAMILY WOULD BE PROTECTED BY THE GOVERNMENT.

NET 6 FIGURES, MEANING A DATE WAS SET FOR THIS BUT NO TIME WAS GIVEN. THE PERSONS IN THIS ROBBERY WERE MYSELF, CHARLES

FERNANDO FLORES

Several years later Fernando returned to the court room to testify again. He was subpoenaed, forced from his home in Florida, where he was living at the time, to return to New Jersey and address his changed statements. During the Rule 33 hearing, Fernando again changed his story, bringing the case back to the prosecutor's favor. Joseph believes that the government threatened Fernando and that was why he changed his testimony again:

Direct Examination, Rule 33 Hearing: July 10, 2003
Mr. Berman, Defense Attorney for Joseph Rodriguez:
Q. We're happy to have you.
Do you recall that at the time of trial you testified for the government?
A. Yes.

Q. And I expect that in advance of your testimony you met with the government on numerous occasions?

A. Yes.

Q. How many times did you meet with the government?
A. I don't know. Several.

Q. More than five?

A. Yes.

Q. More than ten?

A. Probably.

Q. More than fifteen?

A. Could have been 100 times, sir, I don't remember exactly how many.

Q. With whom did you meet on behalf of the government? A. With Stu Rabner and with Jim Walsh, John Tamm-I don't remember all their names. I'm sorry.

Q. Who is John Tamm?

A. FBI agent.

Q. When you testified at trial, you testified for a number of days? A. Something like that, yes.

Q. Do you recall how many days you testified for? A. No.

Q. Was it more than two?

A. I think so, yeah.

Q. Was it three?

A. Sir, I don't remember exactly how many days. It's a couple

years back.

Q. When you testified, did you meet with the government in the morning before you got on the stand?

A. I don't remember. I probably did.

Q. Did you meet with the government after you testified at the end of the day after you would testify?

A. I don't remember. I'm not sure. I probably did. I'm not sure.

Q. Where were you staying at the time you testified?

A. I was living in Florida, but I was staying at a hotel at the time of the trial.

Q. How did you get back and forth to the courthouse?

A. I drove with them in the morning.

Q. I'm sorry?

A. I drove with them in the morning.

Q. You drove--

A. Drove with the U.S. Attorney or FBI agent, whoever was there.

Q. So you were chauffeured back and forth to the courthouse?

A. Yes.

Q. Which agent was that?

A. John Tam-I'm not Jim Walsh. I'm sorry.

Q. Agent Walsh drove you back and forth to the courthouse every day?

A. Yes.

Q. Did any of those conversations have to do with the substance of the trial?

A. I don't remember. Could have.

Q. What other things did you talk about with Special Agent Walsh?

A. Talked about a lot of things.

Q. Give one example.

How was Florida, how was the kids doing, how was the new car I had at the time.

Q. So you remember talking to Special Agent Walsh about those things?

A. Yes.

Q. Do you recall talking to Special Agent Walsh about the trial?

A. We could have. Lots of time went to dinner from here. We might have said a few things about the trial, I don't remember.

Q. And were you at that time reluctant to testify?

A. I didn't want to.

Q. In exchange for your testimony, did you receive any promises from the government?

A. No.

Q. Did you receive money?

A. Reward money, yeah.

Q. Say that again.

A. Reward money, yeah.

Q. How much was that?

A. I don't remember the total. I received partial of some and, you know, I don't know what was the total amount.

Q. When did you receive that some?

A. Throughout the trial, I believe. Could have been after, during. I'm not too sure. Could have been before. I don't remember specific dates when I received the money.

Q. Now, you said it could have been before, during and after. Take a minute and think about it.

A. Some money could have been before trial, some money could have came during the trial, and some after. I'm not sure.

Q. Do you think you received money during all those time periods?

A. Could have, yeah. I'm not too sure of that.

Q. How much did you say you got?

A. I didn't say. I don't remember.

Q. Was it thousands?

A. Yeah, it was in the thousands, yes.

Q. Tens of thousands?

A. I'm not too sure of that, no.

Q. And some of that money you received after the trial?
Yeah. I could have received some, yeah.

Q. Other than the money, did the government promise-make any other promises to you?

A. No.

Q. They didn't promise you assistance with finding you a
job?

A. They didn't promise that, no. They said they would
help me, but it was never promised.

Q. So the government told you they would help you find
a job?

A. Said they would help me find a job back in law enforcement, yeah.

Q. So other than telling you they'd give you money, and
other than telling you they'd give you a job, what
else did the government tell you they'd do for you in
exchange for your testimony?

A. That's about it.

Q. Do you recognize this document?

A. I believe I wrote it, yes.

Q. Do you recall when you wrote it?

A. The date is right on it, 7/23/2000.

Q. Do you recall writing it on that day?

A. I don't remember writing it on that day, but that's the
date on the document.

Q. If you look at the second page, it says, I Fernando
Flores, am giving this statement on my own free will
without any threats or promises. Is that true?

A. True.

Q. And in the second paragraph on the page you said you testified in federal court as the government's key witness in the case?

A. I don't remember writing that at all.

Q. You don't remember that?

A. No.

Q. Who typed the letter?

A. I have no idea.

Q. Is it based on your statement?

A. Yes.

Q. So let me ask the question again: The first sentence says that you testified in federal court as the government's key witness in the case. Is that true?

A. True.

Q. The second sentence says that during the trial prep for the case, you were shown surveillance photos from one bank in which it showed three armed men wearing dark clothing in the bank lobby. Is that true?

A. That's false. I might have seen the surveillance photo, but I was never shown the surveillance photo of any bank robbery.

Q. You said you didn't type this statement?

A. I don't remember typing this paragraph right here, no.

Q. Do you remember typing any of the paragraphs?

A. Yes.

Q. So tell me, which paragraph did you type?

A. The third one and the one on the last page.

Q. The paragraph on the last page is the paragraph you typed?

A. The third paragraph on the second page and the last paragraph on the last page.

Q. What about the first paragraph on the second page?

A. Yeah.

Q. You typed that one?

A. I typed that, yeah.

Q. But you typed up to four paragraphs, you typed three of them?

A. I typed three of them.

Q. Did you type the second one?

A. No, I didn't.

Q. And is that paragraph based on the statements you made to either Denise Rodriguez or Lisa Evans?

A. I guess, yes.

Q. So even though you didn't type the second paragraph, it is based upon statements you made?

A. Yes.

Q. So you told either Denise Rodriguez or Lisa Evans that you were shown surveillance photos from the bank?

A. I told them what they wanted to hear to keep peace in the family, yes, I did.

Q. Isn't it true that you shared these statements with Lisa Evans?

A. We talked about the case, yeah, but I don't remember.

Q. When you said, read in the paper, were you reading the paper before the trial?

A. Yes.

Q. And isn't it true you were asked at trial as to whether you had read newspaper reports?

A. Yes.

Q. What did you answer?

A. I said, no.

Q. Was that true?

A. No. I did read articles in the paper about the case, yes.

Q. So that testimony is false?

A. Yes.

Q. And--

The Court: Can you ask him about the timing of reading those newspaper accounts before, during or after trial?

Mr. Brman: Sure.

Q. I think you just testified-I may have missed it- you read those newspaper articles before the trial commenced?

A. I was told not to read any during the trial, anything pertaining to the case. I did read some articles in the paper, yeah.

Q. You read articles regarding the robberies?

A. Bank robberies, yeah.

Q. Prior to trial?

A. Yes.

Q. Let me ask you, Mr. Flores, when you met with the government to prepare your testimony, did Special Agent Walsh show you surveillance photos of the bank robberies?

A. No, he did not.

Q. Did you see surveillance photos of the bank robberies?

A. I seen one surveillance photo of a bank robbery, but I don't know if it had pertained to this case or not.

Q. And whose office were you in?

A. It was, I guess, in the FBI building in Cherry Hill.

Q. And there was a surveillance photo in the room?

A. You walk in the room, there was a photo of three guys, which I don't know, looked like a surveillance photo from the bank It was laying up against the wall. I walked in the room, they saw, took it out of the room. They said I'm not supposed to see that, or whatever. I stared. At that stage, they said specifically for this case. I walked in the room, I looked at it, they took it away.

Q. But you saw it?

A. Yes.

Q. So when you wrote in this statement that you were shown F.B.I. reports, that was a lie?

A. That was a lie, yes.

Q. And when you write that you saw surveillance photos in this statement, it was a lie?

A. In this statement, it's a lie, yes. After hearing Fernando Flores' testimony during the hearing, Judge Greenway determined that there were no grounds for a reversal. Fernando did admit to lying to Lisa C. Evans during his interview with her, but he maintained during the Rule 33 hearing that his trial testimony was true. Judge Greenway felt that nothing he heard during the hearing debunked Fernando's trial testimony, leaving Joseph Rodriguez nothing to argue. The conviction was up held, and no new trial was granted.

CHAPTER 37

Was Fernando credible? Is Joseph Rodriguez's contention true that Fernando was specifically coached by the government and given information that he did not originally have just to sustain a conviction? According to Denise Rodriguez, Joseph's girlfriend, Fernando always testified officially on the government's behalf, because he was afraid that the government would kill him if he didn't. Can we accept that statement as true or false? We may never know for sure. Joseph Rodriguez still maintains his innocence in the bank robbery case. He is trying to fight to regain his freedom.

Fernando Flores will never be able to tell anyone what he thinks anymore. On Friday, July 13, 2007, Fernando died of drug overdose. Joseph Rodriguez believes that the guilt of what Fernando did to his own family was just too much for him to endure.

Whether Fernando was a credible witness is an issue for concern. Liar or not, a jury convicted the three defendants using Fernando's testimony as their main evidence. But was this sentence justified in all of its harshness, or is there something more inhumane at the center of the conclusion of this case?

The answer is still up for debate. Amongst the pantheons of law and civil rights advocates, a silent battle wages in regards to sentencing schemes used by the Federal Courts. It is a very complicated war. The particulars of the system called, the United States Sentencing Guidelines (U.S.S.G.) and the United States Code (U.S.C.) can get confusing.

To keep things as simple as possible, the only subject to be outlined will be what's called, 18 United States Code (U.S.C.), 924 (c). The 18 (U.S.C). 924(c) statute is just one title that was charged in the indictment, but it's the most damaging charge.

And the most controversial.

The 924 (c) counts are charges arising from gun violations. For Charles and Joseph Rodriguez, counts 3, 5, and 8 are 924 (c) charges. Each one of these counts describes a gun violation. 924 (c), in its simplest form, states that the first conviction under a 924 (c) count is 60 months. (Depending on the manner in which the gun is used and the type of gun. These factors alter the minimum mandatory sentence allowed.) Any 924 (c) conviction after the first one currently carries a mandatory 25 years consecutive sentence to each other and any and all other counts.

At the time Joseph Rodriguez was facing his charges, the 924 (c) statute called for a "20" year consecutive sentence for all 924 (c) convictions after the first one. The statute was later amended from "20" years for the second subsequent 924 (c) conviction, to "25" for the second subsequent 924 (c) conviction. The Rodriguez brothers fell under the older statute where "20" years was the mandatory sentence for the second and subsequent 924 (c) conviction.

Because of the consecutive sentencing scheme of 924 (c), counts 3 and 5 alone equal 300 months (25 years) and count 8 requires a life sentence because of the type of weapons possessed and used in the crime. Just for counts 3,5, and 8, the mandatory umbers from the 924 (c) statute are extremely high. Some people even consider the 924 (c) statute to be unfair.

Being convicted of the two bank robberies and the attempted robbery of the armored car exposed the Rodriguez brothers to such a harsh penalty. Under a system that could be considered more fair, the Rodriguez brothers would have received 175 months (approximately 14 years plus an extra 60 months (5 years) or 120 months (10 years) for the gun violations.) That adds up to 20-25 years. For a crime that did not result in the death of anyone or serious injury, 25 years in prison could be considered adequate punishment.

Jose E. Soto, who was acquitted of the two bank robbery allegations, received 37 years just for his participation in the government coordinated Walt Whitman Plaza incident. An attempted robbery of an armored car that never existed.

Jose only had one 924 (c) count, that was count 8. That one count alone earned him a 30 year sentence. Because of the mandatory consecutive sentencing of the 924 (c) counts, Jose received an extra 7 years from the other 3 related counts.

Does a 37 sentence stand firm on the true purpose of our justice system, to "rehabilitate"? Would a 20 year sentence be sufficient enough to properly punish Jose Soto for being guilty on four criminal counts of an indictment?

Unfortunately, as it stands, the 924 (c) sentencing methods practiced by the federal courts have devastated the lives of many defendants and their families. Although society may believe in the harsh punishment under the 924 (c) gun violation statute, in a civil rights case, and under the

United States Constitution, the 924 (c) statute has surely fallen beneath the American standards of justice and fairness.

The sentencing frenzy created by the 924 (c) statute has allowed the enforcers of our legislative bodies of law to lose sight of the true purpose of punishment and our prison system. Our criminal justice system was honorably conceived and constructed to punish the violator in a just manner. It was meant to rehabilitate and prepare our prisoners to re-enter the free world as a productive member of society.

Somewhere along the way, this initiative has been lost. One can truly question the fairness and integrity of our modern legal system. Just look at the F.B.I.'s method of operation in collaring a wanted fugitive. Some might say that they went beyond their call of duty. Instead of continuing their search and investigation as to the whereabouts of Charles Rodriguez. They conceived an elaborate scheme that involved a total of four human lives. Three of those men were nothing more than pawns. They were three more men than the F.B.I, initially wanted. The F.B.I., set in motion preparations for a phony robbery. An operation initiated by one of their own operatives, Fernando Flores, making the F.B.I, official co-conspirators in the attempted armored car robbery.

If, as Brenda Bennet testified to in her deposition, the government did supply Fernando with the guns named in the indictment, then should they be allowed to demand the full punishment under penalty of the 924 (c) violations? If the government pre-determined the outcome of the case by supplying specific weapons that would knowingly trigger a specific mandatory sentence, are they justified in their pursuit of those mandatory sentences?

Did the government induce the three defendants to commit a greater crime than what they might have committed without the government's involvement; if, in fact, the defendants would have committed any crime at all?

The defendants sure felt that the government shouldn't have been rewarded the full penalties of the 924 (c) counts after such an elaborate setup. All three defendants joined together in a motion to urge the court to consider the sentencing entrapment perpetrated by the F.B.I.

Judge Joseph A. Greenway Jr. denied to consider the sentencing entrapment argument and sentenced all of the defendants according to the statutory interpretation commonly used for 924(c) violations.

However, another judge in a separate case believed quite differently than Judge Greenway on the subject of sentencing entrapment.

In the case, United States v Grant. 524 F. Supp. 2d 1204 (C.D. Cal. 2007), defendants Lamont Dinkins and Sanco Grant III were both indicted for conspiracy to distribute cocaine base, and distribution of cocaine base. A former acquaintance of Dinkins contacted him to make an order for four and a half ounces of cocaine. It just so happen that Dinkins' acquaintance was a confidential witness for the F.B.I.

Dinkins and Grant met the confidential witness and made the sale of four and a half ounces of crack. Under the statute for cocaine base, four and a half ounces of crack triggers a mandatory minimum sentence of ten years in prison. The government pushed for the ten year minimum sentence, but Grant contested the sentence. The fact that the confidential witness working for the Federal Bureau of Investigation initiated the buy of four and a half ounces of crack on behalf of the F.B.I. posed a problem.

District Judge Spencer Letts presided over the case. In his decision, he commented, that, "The court's conclusion is not based on the fact that the government instigated and participated in the criminal conspiracy that produced the defendant's conviction, but rather that it claimed unilateral control over those persons." (76)

The word "unilateral" means, "... or done by one side only." The judge acknowledged the fact that the F.B.I. (government) had control of the elements of the crime since the inception of the sting, much like the circumstances in the Rodriguez case.

His Honorable Judge Spencer Letts further goes on to say in his opinion, "... the government maintained unilateral control from the beginning to end over both of the defendants' sentences. The government instigated the sting by tricking Dinkins, (Rodriguez bro.) and Grant (Soto) into participating in what would appear to be a bonafide drug sale. (Robbery). The government could have obtained criminal convictions by arranging to have Grant (Soto) and Dinkins (Rodriguez Bro. participate in any sale of any controlled substance (Robbery) in a distributable amount. (Using any type of firearm). Notwithstanding that, the government as the instigator predetermined that the drug to be bought and sold would be crack cocaine and that amount would be sufficient to trigger the minimum." (77)

In the Rodriguez/Soto case, Brenda Bennet testified in her deposition that, "...The F.B.I, supplied those guns to Fernando." If this is true, then as the government pre-determined the sentencing outcome in the Grant case by being sure a certain amount of crack was sold, so it is with the Rodriguez brothers. Where the government (F.B.I.) allegedly supplied Fernando with weapons to use for the phony robbery setup, their mandatory sentencing scheme under 924 (c), and therefore participated in sentencing entrapment.

Furthermore, the judge in the Grant case states, "Once the government set the sting in motion, therefore, it guaranteed that if it was successful, Grant and Dinkins (Rodriguez bro. and Soto) would be pre-sentenced by the government to a prison term of ten years..."(78)

Ultimately, Judge Spencer Letts refused to sentence Grant to the mandatory minimum sentence in that case because the government's setup operation (sting) unfairly pre-determined the sentence against a person who otherwise was not predisposed to commit such an act.

Although the government in the Rodriguez/Soto case brought charges of armed bank robbery against the defendants, their case depended on testimony given by their confidential witness. Fernando Flores' identity may have been revealed during the trial, but it is undisputed that he was instrumental in the government's sting operation. Even more damaging is the fact that in his own deposition with Lisa C. Evans, he admitted that the F.B.I provided detailed information concerning the bank robberies. Fernando may have recanted his statement, again, during the Rule 33 hearing, but it does not erase the questions that have risen concerning his credibility or change the undeniable fact of his participation as a government confidential witness.

"One of the fundamental rights protected by the Bill of Rights is the individual right to liberty protected by the Due Process Claus. The Due Process Claus provides heightened protection against arbitrary and unreasonable infringements of liberty by the government. "(79) The 924 (c) statutes used to sentence the Rodriguez brothers and Jose Soto, among others, has belittled entirely the meaning of the Due Process Claus. No person ever died, no person ever sustained serious injury in the bank robberies, yet the Rodriguez brothers were sentenced to life in prison, where in some states a cold blooded murderer can be home in twenty years.

Soto was acquitted of all the bank robberies, but simply because he was present during the one phony robbery, setup by the F.B.I., he will be spending the better part of 37 years of his life behind bars. Yet he, too, maintained steady work and paid his bills like any other working citizen. At the time of the incident, his wife was pregnant with twins. Now his children will never know him except through a set of bars.

Does Soto deserve to spend so much time in prison? A cut of one million dollars is hard to resist when it's constantly shoved in your face, even for the most honorable person.

It is agreed that those who commit crimes must pay their debt to society. There cannot be social order without punishment for the disruption of that order. But at the same token, there is a fairness and reasonableness standard that must be maintained. At one time, those two fundamental ideas were what separated the United States of America from so many other ruthless and unfair countries.

Without the fairness and reasonableness standard present in our judicial system, the United States of America is dangerously approaching the edge of adopting the mannerisms of the monster governments that it professes to protect its citizens from.

It can be said, without question that the sentencing methods used by the federal court in the Rodriguez/Soto case, mainly the 924 (c)'s, were extremely excessive. For a man to be sentenced to life in prison and not have taken a life of another is far from the intended purpose of the formers of our Constitution and judicial system. That purpose is "rehabilitation".

Joseph Rodriguez and Soto were both men who worked their everyday jobs just like any other citizen. Although Joseph served time for manslaughter, he paid his debt to society and was released. He returned to the free world and integrated himself as a productive part of society. He worked full time for a landscaping company and bought a home for himself and his small family. With Jose Soto as a co-worker at the landscaping company, the two did their best to provide for their families.

It is true that Jose Soto and Joseph Rodriguez both worked regularly. It can be argued if the two were already predisposed to committing such a crime like the armored car robbery at the rest stop. Would they have participated in something of that magnitude without the influence of Fernando Flores? The question remains, was the F.B. I. justified in their tactics used to snare a wanted fugitive by setting into motion an elaborate set-up involving two individuals who, had it not been for the persistence of the F.B.I.'s confidential witness, probably would not have engaged in such a plan? And, can the F.B.I, truly be justified for allowing the phony robbery to proceed when they had their intended target, Charles Rodriguez, cornered at Fernando's apartment long before the rest stop incident was to happen that same morning.

It can be said that the authorities had a personal interest in the fate of Charles Rodriguez. He was wanted for the attempted murder of a Camden County Police officer. The idea to rob an armored car was conceived to bring Charles Rodriguez out of hiding using his brother as bait. The special interest in Charles Rodriguez may have clouded the judgment of the agents involved.

The entire scheme was hatched by the F.B.I., to apprehend, or as stated by Fernando Flores, assassinate Charles

Rodriguez for shooting Officer Leoni III. Many lives were upended and destroyed because of the government's conquest for one man.

Charles Rodriguez eventually faced trial for the shooting of Officer Leoni III. As mentioned before, the hype surrounding Charles Rodriguez throughout the media was found to be less than accurate. In the end, on December 12, 2000, Charles Rodriguez was found not guilty on all counts charging him with the shooting.

All of the drama and hardship was created to bring the shooter of Officer Leoni III to justice. Charles Rodriguez was supposedly that man. But a jury found that Charles was not involved in the shooting of the officer. Unfortunately, the trial for the shooting was held after, the Rodriguez brothers and Soto were sentenced for the robberies.

The authorities slandered Charles Rodriguez's name all over the media. They set into motion a large sting operation to bring down one man. Charles Rodriguez was the focus of their revenge for Officer Leoni III getting shot. Yet Charles Rodriguez had nothing to do with that shooting. Still, he and two other men will be spending the remainder of their lives in prison.

FEDERAL PUBLIC DEFENDER
DISTRICT OF NEW JERSEY

800 HUDSON SQUARE, SUITE 350
CAMDEN NEW JERSEY 08102
(609) 757-5341 Telephone
(609) 757-1273 Facsimile

RICHARD COUGHLIN
FEDERAL PUBLIC DEFENDER

TONIANNE J. BONGIOVANNI
FIRST ASSISTANT

March 11, 1999

- Hand Delivered -

Honorable Joseph A. Greenaway, Jr.
United States District Judge
District of New Jersey
King Building, Room 4040
50 Walnut Street, P.O. Box 999
Newark, NJ 07101-0999

Re: United States v. Charlie Rodriguez, Joseph Rodriguez and
Jose Soto, Criminal No. 98-547 (JAG)
EMERGENCY MOTION FOR INJUNCTIVE RELIEF

Dear Judge Greenaway:

Please be advised that it has come to our attention that a government witness, Fernando Flores, has been assaulting & harassing a potential defense witness, Brenda Bennet in the above referenced case. Additionally, we also have reason to believe that two FBI agents intimidated the same witness at her place of employment.

As a result of the actions by government witness Flores, Ms. Bennet obtained a restraining order and has filed several other complaints against Mr. Flores. Furthermore, Ms. Bennet feels threatened by Mr. Flores and is in fear of her life. Additionally, despite the restraining order, Mr. Flores has made several attempts to speak with Ms. Bennet by giving messages to third parties. Ms. Bennet believes that the assaults made on her by Mr. Flores are a result of Mr. Flores believing that she has had contact with defendants' investigators regarding the matter of United States v. Charlie Rodriguez, et al.

In addition to the assaults on Ms. Bennet , Mr. Flores assaulted a juvenile relative of Joseph and Charlie Rodriguez and subsequently harassed him as well.

The following is a list of facts in support of Defendant Jose Soto's claim that Fernando Flores, a government witness, as well as government agents, have committed obstruction of justice and intimidation of a potential defense witness:

23 South Clinton Avenue, Station Plaza #4, 4th Floor, Trenton, New Jersey 08609 (609) 989-2160

972 Broad Street, Newark, New Jersey 07102 (973) 645-6347

241

1.   January 19, 1999. Investigators representing the defendants Jose Soto and Joseph Rodriguez, made contact with Brenda Bennet   a potential witness in the matter of U.S. v. Charlie Rodriguez, et al.

2.   January 19, 1999. After informing Mr. Flores of the contact made by defendants' investigators, an argument between Mr. Flores and Ms. Bennet   ensued and became physical. Fernando Flores assaulted Brenda Bennet   outside of his apartment in Merchantville, New Jersey. Mr. Flores body slammed Ms. Bennet   sprayed her with mace, and threatened her with a baseball bat. A criminal complaint was filed under case number S1999-06-0424 and a Temporary Restraining Order (TRO) was issued by the Municipal Court of Merchantville. TRO Attached as Exhibit A(1-4).

3.   January 20, 1999. Palmyra, New Jersey. Brenda Bennet   noticed her car had been tampered with. Things were missing and 6 fuses were disconnected. Ms. Bennet   believed that Fernando Flores tampered with the automobile. A complaint was filed with the Palmyra police. As a result, two warrants were issued for the arrest of Mr. Flores by the Palmyra Police Department.(W1999-39-0328 and W1999-40-0328). Flores was charged with violation of a restraining order and criminal mischief. Domestic Violence Offense Report attached as Exhibit B(1-11). Subsequently on January 21, 1999, Flores was arrested by Merchantville Police on the outstanding Palmyra warrants. Complaint attached as Exhibit C(1-2).

4.   January 21, 1999. The Camden County Superior Court issued a restraining order against both Fernando Flores and Brenda Bennet   not to have contact with each other.

5.   January 22, 1999. Ms. Bennet   brakes failed which caused her to have a car accident. Ms. Birchfield was informed that it appeared someone had tampered with her brakes.

6.   January 29, 1999. Agents Jim Walsh and Peter Loscalzo appeared on the job of Ms.Bennet   unannounced and flashing their badges. Several of Ms. Bennet   's co-workers witnessed the agents approach her. The agents then questioned her about defendants' investigators' inquiry of her, what she told defendants' investigators and whether she knew anything about Fernando's involvement with Joseph and Charlie Rodriguez. The agents also stated that they did not like the fact that Ms. Bennet   was friends with Marissa Rivera, the sister of Joseph and Charlie Rodriguez. Furthermore the agents told Ms. Bennet   not to tell the defendants' investigators anything and that she did not have to talk to them.

7.   March 6, 1999. Fernando Flores assaulted Brenda Bennet   and Michael Rivera, the fifteen year old son of Marissa Rivera. Ms.Bennet   and Michael were in her vehicle. Mr. Flores grabbed Michael and pushed him to the ground. Mr. Flores then grabbed Ms. Bennet   while she was in her car, pulled her hair, choked her and attempted to punch her. In his attempt to punch Ms. Bennet   l, Mr. Flores damaged the rear view mirror of Ms. Bennet   car. He also destroyed her pager. Consequently, complaints were filed by Michael Rivera and Brenda Bennet   Incident Report attached as Exhibit D(1-4).

8.   March 7, 1999. Fernando Flores followed Michael Rivera home Sunday in threatening manner. Mr. Flores was in a vehicle and Michael was a pedestrian. Michael fe threatened by Mr. Flores presence because of the assault incident which occurred on Saturday March 6, 1999. Michael is now afraid to leave his home

Ms. Bennet   and the Rivera family are traumatized over the recent incidents and ar seeking immediate relief. Therefore, the defense is requesting an immediate injunction restrainin Mr. Flores from having any contact with Brenda Bennet   , Michael Rivera and any other famil members of Jose Soto, Joseph Rodriguez, and Charlie Rodriguez. In addition, government agent should be restrained from having any improper contact or improper communications wit witnesses.

The defense also requests a hearing to determine whether Mr. Flores acted with knowledg and consent of the federal law enforcement agents when he attempted to intimidate Ms. Bennet This is necessary to determine whether prosecutorial misconduct has occurred. At this time counsel has no way of knowing what promises have been made to Mr. Flores or whether he is stil acting as a government agent. To the extent that the government was unaware of Mr. Flores criminal conduct, this will also serve to put them on notice with respect to the efforts he ha undertaken on their behalf.

Please contact me if you need any additional information or material.

Respectfully submitted,

LISA C. EVANS
Assistant Federal Public Defender
Counsel for Jose Soto

DAVID A. HOLMAN
Assistant Federal Public Defender
Counsel for Jose Soto

cc   Howard Wiener, Assistant United States Attorney
Stuart Rabner, Assistant United States Attorney
Wayne Powell, Esquire
Martin Isenberg, Esquire

Interview with Joseph Rodriguez

Friend: Hello Joe. How are you today?

Joseph Rodriguez: I'm good. Thanks.

Friend: I wanted to ask you a couple of questions to give the readers a little insight on who you are.

Joe: Okay, shoot.

Friend: Where were you born?

Joe: Camden New Jersey. I was born at Cooper Hospital, on October 22, 1967.

Friend: What can you say about your life growing up?

Joe: I had a, you know, we were poor. It was rough sometimes. Friend: Did you complete High School or get your G.E.D.? Joe: I had to go to summer school, but I did end up getting my diploma.

Friend: How do you describe yourself as a man?

Joe: I think I'm a nice guy. I'm easy to get along with. I like to have fun. I'm a jokester. I don't take things to seriously, and I can let things just roll off my shoulders.

Friend: Since your conviction, how long have you been in prison? Joe: 11 years. We got setup in 1998.

Friend: Tell the readers about the efforts you have made to try to bring this case back around for you.

Joe: Well, I've hired investigators to go to the rest stop. I have had Investigators check bank photos. My family had to track down Fernando's girlfriend. I've studied the law a little to understand my case and talked with guys in jail who are pretty good with this stuff. I've written hundreds of letters to different people and organizations to try and get some help. I'm constantly working on this thing to salvage some of my life. Friend: Why did you decide to get this book made?

Joe: I don't care about money. I don't want a dime. Sole purpose of this book is I want the truth to come to light good or bad, I don't care about what people say. I just want the truth to be known. I believe the truth can help me a great deal. Friend: What do you hope to accomplish with this book?

Joe: I'm hoping that people will realize how far the F.B.I., government, went to capture Charlie when at the end of it all he was found innocent of the shooting of the officer, which was the cause of the whole phony robbery scheme. Now we're doing all this time because of something they made up from the beginning.

Friend: Thank you Joe for informing the readers. I hope things work out for you in the end.

Joe: Thanks.

Contact the Author

The federal system has a policy of transferring inmates for whatever reason they deem necessary. You can also go to the internet, type in WWW.BOP.GOV, type in my name and number to locate me.

My information is:
    Joseph Rodriguez #20260-050

Feel free to write me.

Enjoy the book, and pass it on to anyone that you feel may be able to help in this matter.
"The Truth is Out There"!

Forgive Me for What I Have Done By Joseph Rodriguez
I did not know what I wanted in life.
When I was young, I didn't care about my own life.
So caring about someone else was not a question that needed to be answer. After making a lot of mistakes, I found

two things that touched my heart so deeply, that all I wanted was to be them and only them.

First, a loving husband with all my heart. Second, a caring father to the little guys in my life. Looking back to the many people I have hurt, some in ways that can never be repaired. No money or words will remove the pain. I can only pray that God will remove it for me, replacing it with his love and peace.

Knowing what I know today will give me the strength to move forward and cause no more pain to those around me.

Forgive me for what I have done!

Source Log

1   Report of Investigation- U.S. V Joseph Rodriguez, File #98-2002 Marissa Rivera, Tues. 12/29/98; pg. 2 par. 1
2   Report of Investigation- U.S. V Joseph Rodriguez, File #98-2002 Marissa Rivera, Tues. 12/29/98; pg. 2 par. 1
3   Report of Investigation- U.S. V Joseph Rodriguez, File #98-2002 Marissa Rivera, Tues. 12/29/98; pg. 2 par. 3
4   Report of Investigation- U.S. V Joseph Rodriguez, File #98-2002 B.B. Mon. 1/25/99; pg. 1 par. 3
5   Report of Investigation- U.S. V Joseph Rodriguez, File #98-2002 B.B. Mon. 1/25/99; pg. par. 3
6   Deposition of B.B.U.S. V Rodriguez/Soto, 1/27/00; Pg. 5 line 25, cont. to pg. 6, line 1.
7   Report of Interview-U.S. V Jose Soto, #98-547; pg. 1 par. 2. 8   Report of Interview-U.S. V Joseph 1/25/99 pg. 2, par. 1.
9   Report of Interview-U.S. V Joseph 1/25/99 pg. 2 par. 3
10 Report of Interview-U.S. V Joseph Rodriguez, #98-2002,
    Rodriguez, #98-2002,
    Rodriguez, #98-2002, 1/25/99; pg. 2, par. 2 11   Deposition Line 13-14. 12   Deposition Line 1.
    13   Deposition Line 5.
    of B.B.-U.S. V Rodriguez/Soto, 1/27/00; pg. 8
    of B.B.-U.S. V Rodriguez/Soto, 1/27/00; pg. 9
    of B.B.-U.S. V Rodriguez/Soto, 1/27/00; pg. 9

14 Report of Interview-U.S. V. Jose Soto, Criminal
    #98-547
    2/1/99;pgs. 1-2, par. 4 and 1.
15 Report of Investigation-U.S. V Joseph Rodriguez, File
    # # 2002, 1/25/99; pg. 2 par. 1
16 Interview, Lisa C, Evans/ Fernando Flores-6/21/00;
    pg. 18, Lines 19-22.
17 Report of Investigation-U.S. V Joseph Rodriguez, File
    File 2002,12/29/98; pg. 4, par. 6.
18 Report of Investigation-U.S. V Joseph Rodriguez, File
    File 2002,12/29/98; pg. 3, par. 4.
19 Deposition of B.B.-U.S. V Rodriguez/Soto, 1/27/00,
    pg. 27, Lines 15-17.
20 Report of Investigation-U.S. V Joseph Rodriguez, File
    File 2002,1/25/99; pg. 2 par. 3
21 Deposition of B.B.-U.S. V Rodriguez/Soto, 1/27/00,
    pg. 23, Lines 3-4.
22 Deposition of B.B.-U.S. V Rodriguez/Soto, 1/27/00,
    pg. 21 Lines 5-9.
23 Report of Investigation-U.S. V Joseph Rodriguez, File
    File 2002,1/25/99; pg. 2 par. 3
24 Report of Investigation-U.S. V Joseph Rodriguez, File
    File 2002, Marissa Rivera, 12/29/98; pg. 4, par. 5
25 Deposition of B.B.-U.S. V Rodriguez/Soto, 1/27/00,
    pg. 23, Line 20.
    Line 20.
    24, lines 25-1.
27 Deposition of B.B.-U.S. V Rodriguez/Soto, 1/27/00,
    pg. 24, Lines 17-18.
28 Interview, Lisa C. Evans/Fernando Flores6/21/00; pg.
    4, Line 14.
29 Interview, Lisa C. Evans/Fernando Flores6/21/00;
    pgs. 6-7, Lines 25-1 and 2.

30 Report of Investigation-U.S. V Joseph Rodriguez, File File 2002,1/25/99 pg. 3 par. 2

31 Report of Investigation-U.S. V Joseph Rodriguez, File File 2002,1/25/99 pg. 3 par. 2

32 Statement made by Joseph Rodriguez during Interview for this book.

33 Interview, Lisa C. Evans/Fernando Flores- 6/21/00; pg. 9, Lines 5-6.

34 Interview, Lisa C. Evans/Fernando Flores- 6/21/00; pg. 9, Lines 17-18.

35 Interview, Lisa C. Evans/Fernando Flores- 6/21/00; pg. 9, Lines 10-13.

36 Report of Investigation-U.S. V Joseph Rodriguez File File 2002,1/25/99; pg.3, par. 5.

37 Interview, Lisa C. Evans/Fernando Flores6/21/00; pg. 4, Lines 11.

38 Report of Investigation-U.S. V Joseph Rodriguez File File 2002,1/25/99; pg. 4, par. 1.

39 Deposition of B.B.-U.S. V Rodriguez/Soto, 1/27/00; pg. 26, Lines 18-23.

40 Deposition of B.B.-U.S. Line 11.

41 Deposition of B.B.-U.S. Lines 20-21.

42 Deposition of B.B.-U.S. Lines 24-25.

43 Deposition of B.B.-U.S. V Rodriguez/Soto, 1/27/00; pg. 26,
V Rodriguez/Soto, 1/27/00; pg. 19,
V Rodriguez/Soto, 1/27/00; pg. 25,
V Rodriguez/Soto, 1/27/00; pg. 27, Lines 18-24 and pg. 42 line 7-8. 44   Report of Investigation-U.S. 2002,1/25/99; pg. 3, par. 5. 45 Report of Investiga-tion-U.S. 2002,1/25/99; pg. 2, par. 3. 46   Report of Investigation-U.S. V Joseph Rodriguez File File V Joseph Rodriguez File File

V Joseph Rodriguez File File 2002,1/25/99; pg. 2, par. 3 lines 15-17 and 24, and pg., 40, Lines 3-4.

47 Deposition of B.B.-U.S. V Rodriguez/Soto 1/27/00 pg. 28

Lines 8-14

48 Deposition of B.B. U.S. v Rodriguez/Soto. 1/27/00

49 Interview Joseph Rodriguez

50 Interview Joseph Rodriguez

51 Interview Joseph Rodriguez

52 Courier Post 12-12-00

53 Courier Post 9/16/98

54 Interview Joseph Rodriguez

55 Interview Lisa C. Evans/ Fernando Flores 6/21/00 pg. 21 Lines 23-25 pg. 22 line 21-25.

56 Interview Lisa C. Evans/ Fernando Flores 6/21/00 pg. 21

Lines 23-25 pg. 22 line 21-25. Also Fernando Flores statement. On 7/23/05

57 Interview, Lisa C, Evans/ Also Fernando's Statement 7-28-00 58   Gov. Ex. J-210-Transcribed Fernando Flores 6/21/00

witness Statement, 5/28/98, Commerce Bank, Marter Ave. Moorestown N. J; pg. 2, par. 2.

59 Gov. Ex. J-161 Federal 302, 9/9/98

60 Interview, Lisa C. Evans/Fernando Flores- 6/21/00

61 Interview, Lisa line 21.

62 Interview, Lisa line 24.

C, Evans/ Fernando Flores6/21/00; pg. 18,

C, Evans/ Fernando Flores6/21/00; pg. 18,

63 Trial Transcript- June 9, 1999; Day 7.

64 Trial Transcript- June 9, 1999; Day 7.

65 Trial Transcript- June 9, 1999; Day 7

66 Trial Transcript- June 9, 1999; Day 7.

67 Trial Transcript- June 9, 1999; Day 7.
68 Trial Transcript- June 8, 1999; Day 6.
69 Trial Transcript- June 8, 1999; Day 6.
70 Trial Transcript- May 27, 1999; Day 4
71 Trial Transcript-May 27,1999; Day 4.
72 Concurrently-joint and equal together   .
73 Consecutivelyfollowing in served back to back.
    in authority; (to be served regular order; successive (to
    be
74 U.S. V Grant, 524 F. Supp. 2d 1204 (C.D. cal. 2007).
75 U.S. V Grant, 524 F. Supp. 2d 1204 (C.D. cal. 2007).
76 U.S. V Grant, 524 F. Supp. 2d 1204 (C.D. cal. 2007)
77 U.S. V Grant, 524 F. Supp. 2d 1204 (CD. caL 2007).